Let the Word dwell in you.

With *Explore the Bible,* groups can expect to engage Scripture in its proper context and be better prepared to live it out in their own context. These book-by-book studies will help participants—

- grow in their love for Scripture;
- gain new knowledge about what the Bible teaches;
- develop biblical disciplines;
- internalize the Word in a way that transforms their lives.

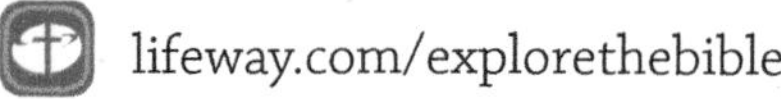

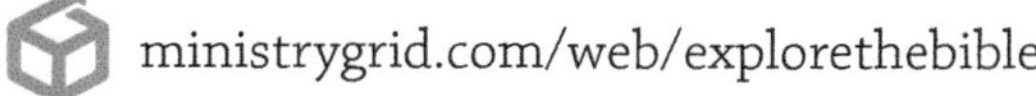

E.
T.

ISBN 978-1-4300-4320-1 • Item 005756894

Dewey decimal classification: 226.9
Subject headings: SERMON ON THE MOUNT \ HEAVEN \ BIBLE. N.T. MATTHEW—STUDY

ERIC GEIGER
Vice President, LifeWay Resources

MICHAEL KELLY
Director, Groups Ministry

GREGG MATTE
General Editor

JEREMY MAXFIELD
Content Editor

Send questions/comments to: Content Editor, *Explore the Bible: Small-Group Study;* One LifeWay Plaza; Nashville, TN 37234.

Printed in the United States of America

For ordering or inquiries visit LifeWay.com; write to LifeWay Small Groups; One LifeWay Plaza; Nashville, TN 37234; or call toll free 800-458-2772.

We believe that the Bible has God for its author; salvation for its end; and truth, without any mixture of error, for its matter and that all Scripture is totally true and trustworthy. To review LifeWay's doctrinal guideline, please visit lifeway.com/doctrinalguideline.

Session 1 quotation: Eleanor Roosevelt, *BrainyQuote.com* [online, cited 13 July 2015]. Available from the Internet: *www.brainyquote.com.* Session 2 quotation: Gregg Matte, *Twitter* [online], 23 February 2015 [cited 13 July 2015]. Available from the Internet: *https://twitter.com/greggmatte.* Session 3 quotation: Martin Luther King Jr., *BrainyQuote.com* [online, cited 13 July 2015]. Available from the Internet: *www.brainyquote.com.* Session 4 quotation: Billy Graham, *BrainyQuote.com* [online, cited 13 July 2015]. Available from the Internet: *www.brainyquote.com.* Session 5 quotation: Corrie ten Boom, *BrainyQuote.com* [online, cited 13 July 2015]. Available from the Internet: *www.brainyquote.com.* Session 6 quotation: Robert Frost, "The Road Not Taken," *Poetry Foundation* [online, cited 13 July 2015]. Available from the Internet: *www.poetryfoundation.org.*

›ABOUT THIS STUDY

WHAT DOES IT LOOK LIKE TO LIVE EACH DAY AS PART OF THE KINGDOM OF HEAVEN?

It's easy to feel that your spiritual life and your practical, day-to-day life are two distinct things. But what if it all blends together into one beautifully unexpected lifestyle in the kingdom of heaven?

Jesus turned over everyone's neat little categories and shattered the traditional understanding of religious teaching. Two opposite extremes had missed the point of a relationship with God. On the one hand, hypocrites used religious activity to build up their own reputations. On the other hand, people genuinely seeking to please God were subject to a burdensome list of rules. But with an authority unlike anyone the crowds had ever heard—and truly unlike any man in history—Jesus intrigued everyone on the mountainside as he described a practical spirituality with surprising implications.

Explore the Bible: Matthew—The Sermon on the Mount reveals with absolute clarity what it means to live each day on earth as part of the kingdom of heaven. This Bible study encourages us to trust in and respond to the loving authority of our Heavenly Father. As part of His kingdom, we bear a family resemblance, reflecting His character throughout the world. Everything we do matters, and the heart motivating our actions is equally important.

The ***Explore the Bible*** series will help you know and apply the encouraging and empowering truth of God's Word. Each session is organized in the following way.

UNDERSTAND THE CONTEXT: This page explains the original context of each passage and begins relating the primary themes to your life today.

EXPLORE THE TEXT: These pages walk you through Scripture, providing helpful commentary and encouraging thoughtful interaction with God through His Word.

OBEY THE TEXT: This page helps you apply the truths you've explored. It's not enough to know what the Bible says. God's Word has the power to change your life.

LEADER GUIDE: This final section provides optional discussion starters and suggested questions to help anyone lead a group in reviewing each section of the personal study.

For helps on how to use *Explore the Bible,* tips on how to better lead groups, or additional ideas for leading, visit www.ministrygrid.com/web/explorethebible.

GROUP COMMITMENT

As you begin this study, it's important that everyone agrees to key group values. Clearly establishing the purpose of your time together will foster healthy expectations and help ease any uncertainties. The goal is to ensure that everyone has a positive experience leading to spiritual growth and true community. Initial each value as you discuss the following with your group.

- [ ] PRIORITY
  Life is busy, but we value this time with one another and with God's Word. We choose to make being together a priority.

- [ ] PARTICIPATION
  We're a group. Everyone is encouraged to participate. No one dominates.

- [ ] RESPECT
  Everyone is given the right to his or her own opinions. All questions are encouraged and respected.

- [ ] TRUST
  Each person humbly seeks truth through time in prayer and in the Bible. We trust God as the loving authority in our lives.

- [ ] CONFIDENTIALITY
  Anything said in our meetings is never repeated outside the group without the permission of everyone involved. This commitment is vital in creating an environment of trust and openness.

- [ ] SUPPORT
  Everyone can count on anyone in this group. Permission is given to call on one another at any time, especially in times of crisis. The group provides care for every member.

- [ ] ACCOUNTABILITY
  We agree to let the members of our group hold us accountable to commitments we make in the loving ways we decide on. Questions are always welcome. Unsolicited advice, however, isn't permitted.

____ _______________

I agree to all the commitments. Date

› GENERAL EDITOR

Gregg Matte has served as the pastor of Houston's First Baptist Church since 2004. Prior to that, he served as the founder, speaker, and director of Breakaway Ministries at Texas A&M University, one of the largest college Bible studies in the nation. What started as a Bible study with 12 participants grew to a weekly gathering of more than 4,000 students.

Gregg is the author of *The Highest Education: Becoming a Godly Man; Finding God's Will: Seek Him, Know Him, Take The Next Step;* and *I AM Changes Who I Am: Who Jesus Is Changes Who I Am, What Jesus Does Changes What I Am to Do.*

Gregg is also a popular speaker at conferences, camps, and retreats across North America. Gregg and his wife, Kelly, have a son, Greyson.

CONTENTS

THE BEATITUDES

Blessings in the kingdom of heaven are reflected in radically countercultural lives today.

ABOUT THE GOSPEL OF MATTHEW

Matthew is the opening book of the New Testament. As such, it is a bridge between the Old and New Testaments. The significance of this fact runs much deeper than mere placement. The Book of Matthew connects with the Old Testament through frequent references to events that are said to fulfill Old Testament promises and prophecies. Matthew's characteristic formula ("All this took place to fulfill what was spoken by the Lord through the prophet") occurs in the opening chapter (1:22) and appears repeatedly. Matthew includes as many as 61 quotations from the Old Testament, about twice that of any other Gospel.

AUTHOR

Although his identity is not disclosed within the Gospel itself, the writer has historically been identified as Matthew (also known as Levi), one of Jesus' twelve disciples. In the earliest known manuscripts his name appeared in the title. Also, the writings of many early church fathers attribute the first Gospel to Matthew.

"HAPPINESS IS NOT A GOAL; IT IS A BY-PRODUCT."

—Eleanor Roosevelt

DATE

Gospel studies have generally agreed that Mark was the earliest of the four Gospels and that Matthew reflects a knowledge of Mark. This consensus suggests that the Matthew was written after Mark. A time of writing in the decade of the 60s would be reasonable.

PURPOSE

Like the other Gospels, Matthew isn't a chronological diary of Jesus' life and ministry. It's a witness to His mission and message. Therefore, events and teachings are arranged with the intent of bearing witness to God's good news brought by His Son. Matthew portrays Jesus as the promised Messiah and the long-awaited King of Israel. In short, in Matthew Jesus is the Messiah-King. This Gospel emphasizes the kingdom of heaven, with Jesus as its Messiah-King. With regard to Jewish sensitivity to using the name of God, Matthew refers to the kingdom only 5 times as the kingdom of God but 32 times as the kingdom of heaven.

MATTHEW 5:1-12

Think About It

***Observe Jesus' repetition of the word* blessed.**

Look for the way each promise is related to the characteristic identified.

1 When He saw the crowds, He went up on the mountain, and
after He sat down, His disciples came to Him. **2** Then He began
to teach them, saying:

3 "The poor in spirit are blessed,
for the kingdom of heaven is theirs.
4 Those who mourn are blessed,
for they will be comforted.
5 The gentle are blessed,
for they will inherit the earth.
6 Those who hunger and thirst for righteousness
are blessed,
for they will be filled.
7 The merciful are blessed,
for they will be shown mercy.
8 The pure in heart are blessed,
for they will see God.
9 The peacemakers are blessed,
for they will be called sons of God.
10 Those who are persecuted for righteousness
are blessed,
for the kingdom of heaven is theirs.

11 "You are blessed when they insult and persecute you and falsely
say every kind of evil against you because of Me. **12** Be glad and
rejoice, because your reward is great in heaven. For that is how
they persecuted the prophets who were before you."

UNDERSTAND THE CONTEXT

USE THE FOLLOWING PAGES TO PREPARE FOR YOUR GROUP TIME.

Religion in Jesus' day was a system of burdensome rules and regulations. The religious leaders, for the most part, were hypocritical and legalistic. Jesus' attitude toward the law of Moses was a refreshing change. He emphasized faithful, sincere obedience instead of a lifeless, ceremonial religion. Jesus sought to bring the focus back to the true messages of the Old Testament prophets recorded in the Scriptures.

Because of their religious leaders' false teachings, the people didn't understand that the ancient prophets were encouraging a heartfelt obedience to God's message and not merely a dutiful observance of laws and rituals.

Matthew 5–7 comprises what's referred to as the Sermon on the Mount. The first section of the sermon, probably the most familiar today, is known as the Beatitudes (see 5:3-10). These words captured the attention of Jesus' disciples and the crowds who were listening. What Jesus said in the Sermon on the Mount demanded a response.

Jesus probably began the Sermon on the Mount while seated among His disciples and other followers on a hillside somewhere around the Sea of Galilee. In the Beatitudes Jesus identified His standards for His followers and promised blessings for those who exhibit His character. Thus, Jesus opened His sermon by telling the people how they could experience true happiness.

› EXPLORE THE TEXT

THE NEW MOSES (Matthew 5:1-2)

1When He saw the crowds, He went up on the mountain, and after He sat down, His disciples came to Him. 2Then He began to teach them, saying ...

Jesus showed compassion for the multitudes who followed Him. People flocked to Him from all levels of society. Among them were the physically sick, emotionally unstable, demon possessed, financially destitute, uneducated, and illiterate. Mingling with this motley crowd were those who were religiously influential and politically powerful. They had no idea that Jesus was the Son of God. But Jesus was different. By nature He was the essence of love, which, like a magnet, drew people to Him. Furthermore, He preached on His own authority, quoting no traditions or great rabbis for His sources. He was the new Moses and yet was totally different from that great lawgiver. Moses descended Mount Sinai with God's law and confronted the people with God's judgment because of their sins. Jesus delivered His message from a mountain, but He emphasized the reality of a loving God who was ready to forgive sin.

What are some characteristics of a speaker who makes you want to listen?

THE NEW BLESSINGS (*Matthew 5:3-12*)

3The poor in spirit are blessed,
for the kingdom of heaven is theirs.
4Those who mourn are blessed,
for they will be comforted.
5The gentle are blessed,
for they will inherit the earth.
6Those who hunger and thirst for righteousness
are blessed,
for they will be filled.
7The merciful are blessed,
for they will be shown mercy.
8The pure in heart are blessed,
for they will see God.
9The peacemakers are blessed,
for they will be called sons of God.
10Those who are persecuted for righteousness are blessed,
for the kingdom of heaven is theirs.

11You are blessed when they insult and persecute you and falsely say every kind of evil against you because of Me. 12Be glad and rejoice, because your reward is great in heaven. For that is how they persecuted the prophets who were before you.

The Beatitudes with which Jesus began His Sermon on the Mount aren't multiple choice. Just as we don't pick and choose which fruit of the Spirit we'll adopt, we also don't select which Beatitudes we'll ask God to help us develop in our lives. The Beatitudes must be taken as a whole, describing the way God's people must live if they expect Christ to be seen in them.

The word *blessed,* which Jesus used with each Beatitude, can mean *happiness.* Typically, we think of happiness as an emotional response that's dependent on circumstances. Jesus' idea of happiness, however, is associated with the truth that God is at work in you at all times. Religion in Jesus' day wasn't associated with happiness in the lives of the people. Many people saw God as a divine Being who was poised to mete out judgment on sinful human beings. The people who heard Jesus preach and teach considered Him a rabbi, but He was in no

KEY DOCTRINE
Education

In Jesus Christ abide all the treasures of wisdom and knowledge.

way like the rabbis who interpreted God's law to them. He began His preaching not with condemnation and a fearful anticipation of judgment to come but with a resounding theme of happiness. Again and again He repeated it. What Jesus preached was indeed good news.

BIBLE SKILL
Notice repeated words or phrases in a Bible passage.

Jesus repeatedly used the word *blessed* in the Beatitudes (as you identified on p. 8). Other important parts of that repeated pattern are the word *are* and the phrase *will be.*

How do the present tense of *are blessed* and the future tense of *will be* help you understand what Jesus was teaching?

In systematic order Jesus described eight character traits that identify true citizens of the kingdom of heaven. He began with the poor in spirit, those who are aware of their total need for God. True happiness comes when people realize they're spiritually bankrupt before God and must rely on His strength. God gladly gives the kingdom of heaven to those who come to Him in humility and faith.

Jesus' second Beatitude addressed the inescapable fact that sadness is going to be a part of life in this imperfect, sinful world. We mourn when we face great sorrow, experience a devastating tragedy, or are forced to accept failure—and the list of things that cause us to mourn is endless. This Beatitude, however, may refer to godly mourning, a true sorrow for our sins that leads to repentance. This kind of mourning brings the comfort of God's grace and forgiveness.

Gentleness was the third Beatitude. Meekness isn't weakness. This word implies humility and trust in God rather than a self-centered attitude. The earth Jesus said the gentle will inherit refers to the new heaven and new earth promised to believers (see Rev. 21:1).

In the fourth Beatitude Jesus implied that spiritual poverty leads to hunger and thirst for righteousness. God's gift of kingdom life is the only genuine satisfaction for those who yearn for true justice, personal righteousness, and salvation.

How are you tempted to make it on your own in certain areas of need rather than seeking God's help and provision?

Jesus' fifth Beatitude focused on mercy. The word *merciful* implies generosity, compassion, and forgiveness. Mercy is a part of God's nature. He forgives sin and shows kindness to the downtrodden. It's second nature for those who've experienced God's mercy to show the same mercy to others.

Purity of heart is the sixth Beatitude. This is single-minded devotion to God. It's the quality of those who are aware of their total need for God, mourn their spiritual poverty, and hunger and thirst for His righteousness. The pure will see God and experience intimate fellowship with Him.

Peacemakers are addressed in Jesus' seventh Beatitude. Peace describes a state of wholeness and completeness in all areas of life, including our relationships with God and others. Those who strive to make peace do the work of God and will be called children of God.

In the final beatitude Jesus dealt with an inevitable fact of life for true followers of Christ: they'll be persecuted. Those who are persecuted because they serve Christ can rejoice because their reward in heaven will be great.

Review the eight characteristics in the Beatitudes. Which one do you believe to be most needed in our world today?

Which one is most needed in your community?

› **OBEY** THE TEXT

Blessings in the kingdom of heaven are reflected in radically countercultural lives today. God's gift of kingdom life is the only genuine satisfaction of those yearning for righteousness.

Reflect on the eight characteristics identified by Jesus in the Beatitudes. In which of these areas are you most openly demonstrating Christ's character?

What actions do you need to take to more faithfully live according to His standards?

As a group, evaluate on a scale of 1 to 5 how well your group demonstrates each of the eight characteristics. Identify the one needing the most attention in your group and develop a plan for improving the demonstration of that characteristic within the group.

MEMORIZE

"Those who hunger and thirst
for righteousness are blessed,
for they will be filled." Matthew 5:6

USE THE SPACE PROVIDED TO MAKE OBSERVATIONS AND RECORD PRAYER REQUESTS DURING THE GROUP EXPERIENCE FOR THIS SESSION.

MY THOUGHTS

Record insights and questions from the group experience.

MY RESPONSE

Note specific ways you'll put into practice the truth explored this week.

MY PRAYERS

List specific prayer needs and answers to remember this week.

SESSION 2

Salt, Light, & Fruit

Our actions reveal allegiance either to our own glory or to the glory of God.

UNDERSTAND THE CONTEXT

USE THE FOLLOWING PAGES TO PREPARE FOR YOUR GROUP TIME.

In Matthew 5:13-16 Jesus explained the outcome when Christians reflect the character of Christ in their lives. He used two common household items, salt and light, to illustrate the influence Christians have in the world. A true disciple makes a difference in the world. The character of Christ can't describe who you are without also affecting what you do.

Likewise, we can recognize the difference between true and false disciples or teachers. In a warning about false prophets (see 7:15-20), Jesus pointed to the quality of a person's life as his credentials. Eloquence, persuasiveness, attractive personalities, popular followings, and powerful deeds aren't the best indicators of genuine spokespersons for God.

Either way, whether the fruit is good or bad, Jesus is clear that a person's actions reveal his or her nature. Children of God produce good fruit, acting in a way that points to their Heavenly Father. Others claim to belong to the kingdom, but the bad fruit they produce is evidence that they live to serve themselves, not Jesus, our King.

"SPIRITUALLY, MANY OF US ARE NOT LIVING COMPLETELY IN THE LIGHT OR IN THE DARK. WE'VE SETTLED FOR A LIFE AT DUSK."

—Gregg Matte

› MATTHEW 5:13-16; 7:15-20

Think About It

Jesus used obvious truths from the natural world to communicate spiritual realities.

List the positive imagery.

List the negative imagery.

5:13 You are the salt of the earth. But if the salt should lose its taste, how can it be made salty? It's no longer good for anything but to be thrown out and trampled on by men. **14** You are the light of the world. A city situated on a hill cannot be hidden. **15** No one lights a lamp and puts it under a basket, but rather on a lampstand, and it gives light for all who are in the house. **16** In the same way, let your light shine before men, so that they may see your good works and give glory to your Father in heaven.

7:15 Beware of false prophets who come to you in sheep's clothing but inwardly are ravaging wolves. **16** You'll recognize them by their fruit. Are grapes gathered from thornbushes or figs from thistles? **17** In the same way, every good tree produces good fruit, but a bad tree produces bad fruit. **18** A good tree can't produce bad fruit; neither can a bad tree produce good fruit. **19** Every tree that doesn't produce good fruit is cut down and thrown into the fire. **20** So you'll recognize them by their fruit.

EXPLORE THE TEXT

NEW EXPECTATIONS (Matthew 5:13-16)

13You are the salt of the earth. But if the salt should lose its taste, how can it be made salty? It's no longer good for anything but to be thrown out and trampled on by men.

Jesus stated that those who exhibit the qualities expressed in the Beatitudes will function as salt and light in the world. This isn't a choice; it's a fact. Those who possess a genuine Christian character are going to impact the world. In His High Priestly prayer, Jesus didn't ask His Father to take His followers out of the world. Rather, He sent them forth to make an impact on the world. His plan was for them to be in the world but not of it (see John 17:15-16).

Salt was very valuable in Jesus' day. The Romans believed that, except for the sun, nothing was worth more than salt. They often paid their soldiers in salt, a practice from which came the saying "Not worth his salt." Salt is a flavoring agent, for certain foods would be tasteless and flat without the proverbial pinch of salt. Salt is also a preservative, absorbing water from foods, making them too dry to support harmful mold or bacteria. Much of the salt used in Jesus' day came from the Dead Sea. The impure salt taken from this area was susceptible to deterioration that left only useless crystals. Such salt couldn't be restored and thus had lost its saltiness. Jesus said it was good for nothing but to be cast out and to be trodden under foot by men. Weak, compromising Christians lose their spiritual flavor to attract unbelievers away from the tasteless, sinful society in which they live.

How can you apply Jesus' teaching on salt to the life of a follower of Christ? How would you describe the spiritual "flavor" of your life?

[14]You are the light of the world. A city situated on a hill cannot be hidden. [15]No one lights a lamp and puts it under a basket, but rather on a lampstand, and it gives light for all who are in the house. [16]In the same way, let your light shine before men, so that they may see your good works and give glory to your Father in heaven.

Jesus came as light into a spiritually dark world, and He expected His disciples to reflect His light. He compared the light of His followers to a city that's set on an hill, whose lights cannot be hidden. Jesus then compared His followers to a candle used to bring light to a darkened house. He pointed out the foolishness of lighting a candle and then putting it under a large bushel (probably a clay jar). Houses in Jesus' day were dark, often having only one small window high on one wall to keep thieves from entering the house. Many had a portable candlestick on which a candle could be placed. The stand could be moved from one location to another in the house, providing light wherever it was needed.

Jesus' disciples were to reflect the light of their Master, who was the Light of the world. The combined lights of the city on the hillside couldn't be hidden. Like lamps lighted in a darkened house, Jesus' disciples must reflect Jesus' light in a dark world. They must no more try to hide their lights in the world than someone would place a clay jar over a lighted lamp, blocking its light. Rather, the light was to shine in the best location so that all people in the house could see. True believers reflect from within them the Lord Jesus, who is the Light of the world.

What other analogies could be used to explain the truth Jesus taught in this passage?

GOOD VERSUS BAD? (Matthew 7:15-20)

[15]Beware of false prophets who come to you in sheep's clothing but inwardly are ravaging wolves. [16]You'll recognize them by their fruit. Are grapes gathered from thornbushes or figs from thistles?

Jesus issued a warning about people masquerading as heralds of truth. His warning formed the context for introducing the imagery of good and bad trees, along with their respective fruit.

Jesus drew a vivid picture of wolves disguised as sheep. Inside the innocent appearance of sheep's clothing lurks a wolf bent on living up to its nature by devouring its prey. Jesus warned His hearers that false prophets often come in disarming disguises. As peddlers of error, false prophets can cause immeasurable havoc among God's flock. It's a warning that should be heeded in every generation and in all places.

In verse 16 Jesus alerted His hearers that false prophets can be recognized by their fruit. God's people must ask, "What's the outcome of a self-styled prophet's work? Does he leave people better than he found them? Does his message promote godliness in the hearers' lives? Does he teach God's truth? Does his private life match his public declarations?" Jesus' message is the same now as it was then: make a careful inspection of the fruit of the prophet's life, message, and motives.

To underscore His point, Jesus asked two agricultural questions, the answer to which should be obvious to everyone: Do people gather grapes from thorns or figs from thistles? The implied answer indicates that just as false prophets don't demonstrate Christlike lives, those who accept their false teachings also don't bring forth crops of Christlike deeds.

What's the responsibility of believers when they observe others producing fruit contrary to what the Bible expects of Christians?

KEY DOCTRINE
Christian Witness

All Christians are obligated to seek to make the will of Christ supreme in their lives and in society.

BIBLE SKILL
Use other Scripture passages to help understand a Bible passage.

In Matthew 7:16-20 Jesus provided the basis by which a believer can discern between true and false prophets: Does the prophet bear good fruit? Several Old Testament texts provide further explanation.

Read Jeremiah 23:13 and Deuteronomy 18:21-22.

What additional insights do these passages contribute to your understanding of how to discern between true and false prophets?

17In the same way, every good tree produces good fruit, but a bad tree produces bad fruit. 18A good tree can't produce bad fruit; neither can a bad tree produce good fruit.

Jesus' illustration from nature moved from thornbushes and thistles to fruit trees. He used language that people who lived in a largely agricultural setting would immediately understand. Every good tree brings forth good fruit. All other factors being equal, the quality of the tree dictates the quality of its fruit.

Jesus went on to observe that the reverse is also true. A good tree can't bring forth evil fruit, nor does a corrupt tree bring forth good fruit. Diseased fruit trees produce flawed fruit. Jesus' point related to His warning about false prophets. A true prophet produces good fruit both in his own life and in his hearers' lives. A false prophet is most likely flawed in his own life and reproduces his flaws in others.

When it comes to discerning false teachers, which would you deem most valuable as your safeguard: (1) studying false religions to become well acquainted with their teachings or (2) studying the words of Jesus so that you can judge what others say against His words?

To what teachers and spiritual leaders do you entrust your mind and heart? How do their lives show the genuine fruit of obedience?

19Every tree that doesn't produce good fruit is cut down and thrown into the fire. 20So you'll recognize them by their fruit.

What's true of fruit trees and false prophets is also true of the rest of us. Our true nature is revealed in the way we live. The quality of our hearts shows up in our attitudes, words, and deeds. All of us face the alternative possibilities of either being good and thus doing good or being bad and thus doing bad. People whose lives are characterized by ungodly acts and attitudes are simply revealing the condition of their hearts.

God knows who the pretenders are, so it's a doomed strategy to play at being a Christian. One day the outer layer will be stripped away, and every heart will be laid bare before God. All the pretenders will ultimately be exposed for their lack of genuine fruit. Bad trees face a bad destiny. Jesus said they'll be hewn down and cast into the fire. The Bible is honest about a final destiny in the lake of fire (see Rev. 20:13-15).

True believers aren't perfect, but their hearts have been changed by God's forgiving love. Consequently, we grieve when we fall short and soon find our way to a time of confession and cleansing. Pretenders most likely don't care that they aren't genuine, but genuine Christians always care when they sin.

While God directly and immediately knows those who are His genuine children, others can know it only by what they observe in a person's life. Deeds demonstrate genuine faith. The inner person is revealed through outward conduct. So good fruit matters. It matters eternally, not as the means of securing salvation but as the proof of being a genuine believer in the Savior.

OBEY THE TEXT

Our actions reveal allegiance either to our own glory or to the glory of God. Following Jesus carries expectations for living in accordance with His standards. Believers are to represent Christ to and in this world by both deed and word.

What can you do to remind yourself of the responsibility to live as salt and light?

List actions you need to take to encourage others in word and deed.

Share ways your Bible study group can minister in positive, loving ways to members who seem to be drifting away or are bearing fruit unbecoming of genuine Christ followers.

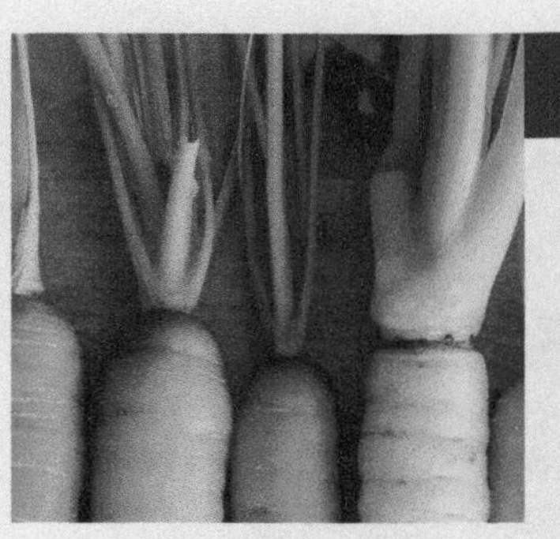

MEMORIZE

"You are the light of the world. A city situated on a hill cannot be hidden."
Matthew 5:14

USE THE SPACE PROVIDED TO MAKE OBSERVATIONS AND RECORD PRAYER REQUESTS DURING THE GROUP EXPERIENCE FOR THIS SESSION.

MY THOUGHTS

Record insights and questions from the group experience.

MY RESPONSE

Note specific ways you'll put into practice the truth explored this week.

MY PRAYERS

List specific prayer needs and answers to remember this week.

SESSION 3

FULFILLING THE LAW

God's Word governs the hearts of His people.

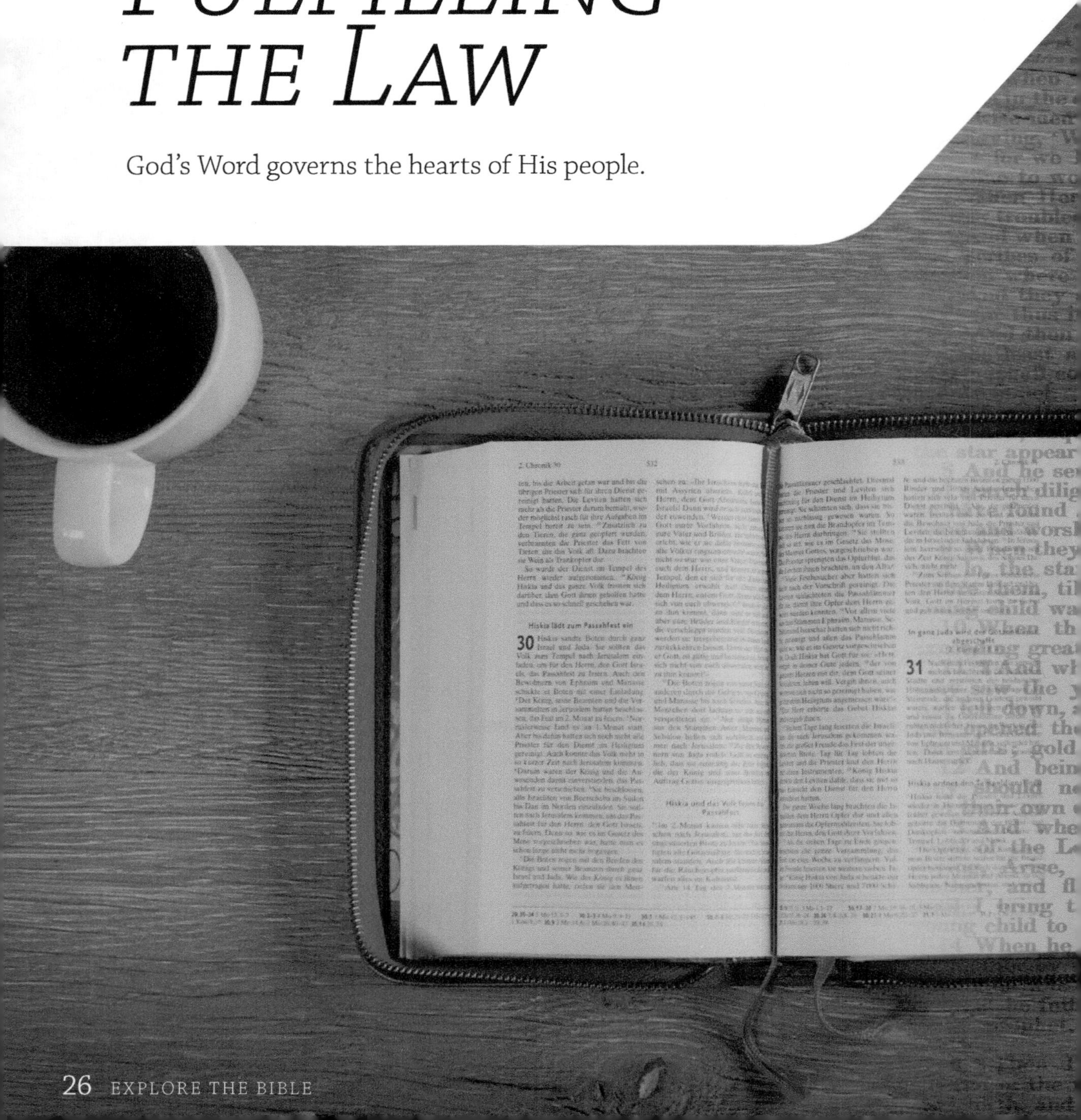

UNDERSTAND THE CONTEXT

USE THE FOLLOWING PAGES TO PREPARE FOR YOUR GROUP TIME.

Throughout the Old Testament are laws God gave to help people better love Him with all their hearts and minds. Their religious leaders had often misquoted and misapplied these laws, reducing them to a mass of rules that could be unintelligible and confusing. Jesus came with a new approach to God's law. He clearly spoke against the abuses and excesses to which the hypocritical religious leaders had subjected it.

Jesus pointed His followers to a higher standard of living than that into which the religious ceremonialism of the day had allowed them to fall. As a result, they'd lost the high view of human life that God's law had emphasized. Brotherly love had degenerated to a level of suspicion and distrust, and love for their enemies was unspeakable. All this led to an inevitable devaluation of others. A basic attitude of selfishness and an unholy sense of pride had seized the people.

In the clearest terms Jesus laid out the way His followers were to approach a lost, sinful world. This way would demonstrate a love that would be redemptive, characterized by a spiritual quality that would draw people to Christ. He taught that it's possible to love sinners without condoning their sin.

"THAT OLD LAW ABOUT 'AN EYE FOR AN EYE' LEAVES EVERYBODY BLIND. THE TIME IS ALWAYS RIGHT TO DO THE RIGHT THING."

—*Martin Luther King Jr.*

› MATTHEW 5:17-22,43-48

Think About It

***Circle each use of the word* heaven.**

In each case underline what Jesus was describing in relation to heaven.

What do these descriptions reveal about the value Jesus placed on these things?

17 Don't assume that I came to destroy the Law or the Prophets. I did not come to destroy but to fulfill. **18** For I assure you: Until heaven and earth pass away, not the smallest letter or one stroke of a letter will pass from the law until all things are accomplished. **19** Therefore, whoever breaks one of the least of these commands and teaches people to do so will be called least in the kingdom of heaven. But whoever practices and teaches these commands will be called great in the kingdom of heaven. **20** For I tell you, unless your righteousness surpasses that of the scribes and Pharisees, you will never enter the kingdom of heaven. **21** You have heard that it was said to our ancestors, "Do not murder," and whoever murders will be subject to judgment. **22** But I tell you, everyone who is angry with his brother will be subject to judgment. And whoever says to his brother, "Fool!" will be subject to the Sanhedrin. But whoever says, "You moron!" will be subject to hellfire.

43 You have heard that it was said, "Love your neighbor" and hate your enemy. **44** But I tell you, love your enemies and pray for those who persecute you, **45** so that you may be sons of your Father in heaven. For He causes His sun to rise on the evil and the good, and sends rain on the righteous and the unrighteous. **46** For if you love those who love you, what reward will you have? Don't even the tax collectors do the same? **47** And if you greet only your brothers, what are you doing out of the ordinary? Don't even the Gentiles do the same? **48** Be perfect, therefore, as your heavenly Father is perfect.

EXPLORE THE TEXT

GREATNESS IN THE KINGDOM (Matthew 5:17-20)

[17]Don't assume that I came to destroy the Law or the Prophets. I did not come to destroy but to fulfill. [18]For I assure you: Until heaven and earth pass away, not the smallest letter or one stroke of a letter will pass from the law until all things are accomplished.

The Law and the Prophets was a title given to written Scripture at the time Jesus was on earth. Because everything Jesus taught during His ministry was based on these Scriptures, we can neither understand nor accept the New Testament apart from the Old. Jesus thus presented this Word of God as the only standard of truth and righteousness. Jesus told His listeners, in no uncertain terms, not to assume that He'd come to destroy the Law and the Prophets but to fulfill them, or to bring out the full meaning of the Scripture, showing that He was the fulfillment of all they prophesied. Jesus would bring the Old Testament promises to their completion.

Jesus used the phrase "I assure you" (v. 18), signaling that what He was about to say was of vital significance. Here He was ascribing the highest authority to God's law. Not only did Jesus fulfill the law, but until the end of the age nothing in God's law would change. God's law is eternally valid, and it will stand until the total plan of God is accomplished. Then, to further strengthen the eternal significance of the law, Jesus said not the smallest letter or the slightest stroke of a pen would disappear from the written law of God until its purpose was completed.

Based on these words of Jesus, how would you describe His view of Scripture?

Why is it important to believe in the inspiration of the Scriptures?

[19]Therefore, whoever breaks one of the least of these commands and teaches people to do so will be called least in the kingdom of heaven. But whoever practices and teaches these commands will be called great in the kingdom of heaven. [20]For I tell you, unless your righteousness surpasses that of the scribes and Pharisees, you will never enter the kingdom of heaven.

After Jesus told His disciples that He'd fulfill and accomplish the entire Law and Prophets, He stressed that His followers were also to keep and practice the commandments. Jesus underscored the grave responsibility that those who teach these commandments must bear. If they don't practice what they teach, they'll be called "least in the kingdom of heaven" (v. 19), whereas those who faithfully practice what they teach will be recognized as great in the kingdom.

Keeping the commandments perfectly was no issue for Jesus, for He was the sinless Son of God. He knew His followers would never reach His level of perfection in this life. Instead, Jesus' emphasis in verse 20 was on the attitude of the heart, not on self-righteous, outer human displays. The Pharisees were satisfied if they outwardly appeared to obey the commandments. They didn't humble themselves before God. True followers of Christ know they can't make themselves righteous enough to enter the kingdom of heaven. Instead, they must depend on God to work His righteousness within them.

What's wrong with the opinion that salvation is achieved and maintained by keeping God's law?

How does self-righteousness differ from the righteousness God desires to see in the lives of His people?

NEIGHBORS IN THE KINGDOM (Matthew 5:21-22)

[21]You have heard that it was said to our ancestors, "Do not murder," and whoever murders will be subject to judgment. [22]But I tell you, everyone who is angry with his brother will be subject to judgment. And whoever says to his brother, "Fool!" will be subject to the Sanhedrin. But whoever says, "You moron!" will be subject to hellfire.

In this context murder meant simply taking innocent life. Various scripture references would exclude capital punishment, justified warfare, killing by accident, and self-defense. The intentional killing of another human being for strictly personal reasons, whatever they may be, violates this commandment. The Pharisees, however, didn't view murder the way Jesus did and the way God intended it to be seen. The Pharisees saw murder only as the physical action of killing.

When Jesus said, "But I tell you" (v. 22), He wasn't nullifying God's commandment or adding His own beliefs. He was simply giving His disciples a more clear understanding of why God made this law to begin with. Moses had written, "Do not murder" (Ex. 20:13). The Pharisees took this command literally and felt righteous because they hadn't literally killed anyone. Although they were angry enough with Jesus to plot His death, they wouldn't perform the physical action of crucifying Him. Jesus was implying that if a person became angry enough to want to kill someone, he or she would have already committed murder in the heart.

Murder is a terrible sin, of course, but anger is also high on the list of grievous sins because it violates God's command to love. Anger, allowed to remain in one's heart, is a dangerous emotion that's always poised and ready to leap out of control. It can lead to mental stress, emotional pain, spiritual distress, and violence. Jesus' words "subject to judgment" (Matt. 5:21) in regard to out-of-control anger had to do with divine judgment, not to the judgment of a human court. In verse 22 Jesus warned that unrighteous anger damages relationships not only between people but also between people and God.

KEY DOCTRINE
The Scriptures

The Holy Bible was written by men divinely inspired and is God's revelation of Himself to people. It is a perfect treasure of divine instruction. It has God for its author; salvation for its end; and truth, without any mixture of error, for its matter. Therefore, all Scripture is totally true and trustworthy.

BIBLE SKILL
Use other Scriptures to help understand a Bible passage.

Jesus said He fulfilled the Law and the Prophets (see Matt. 5:17). Read Matthew 1:22-23; 2:15; 4:14-16. How do these passages affirm Jesus as the One who fulfilled the Old Testament?

Jesus continued this pattern of contrasting traditional understanding with the truth throughout the rest of chapter 5 to explain the inner issues of the heart. In most instances He introduced the accepted teaching with "You have heard that it was said ... ," followed by "But I tell you ..." Jesus left no room for doubt about the way people are to relate to one another within the kingdom of heaven. He went on to address forgiveness (see vv. 23-26), lust (see vv. 27-32), honesty (see vv. 33-37), justice, grace, and humility (see vv. 38-42).

In what way is all behavior, good or bad, ultimately a heart issue?

ENEMIES OF THE KINGDOM (Matthew 5:43-48)

**43You have heard that it was said, "Love your neighbor" and
hate your enemy. 44But I tell you, love your enemies and pray
for those who persecute you, 45so that you may be sons of
your Father in heaven. For He causes His sun to rise on the
evil and the good, and sends rain on the righteous and the
unrighteous. 46For if you love those who love you, what reward
will you have? Don't even the tax collectors do the same? 47And
if you greet only your brothers, what are you doing out of the
ordinary? Don't even the Gentiles do the same? 48Be perfect,
therefore, as your heavenly Father is perfect.**

John 3:16 reminds us that God's love is so great and inclusive that it reaches out to all people, regardless of their sin and rebellion against God. As children of God, we're to reflect the kind of love that He manifests in the world.

We're also reminded of this idea in the Old Testament: "Do not take revenge or bear a grudge against members of your community, but love your neighbor as yourself; I am Yahweh" (Lev. 19:18). The Pharisees took this verse to mean that only those who returned the love they gave were worthy of love. They also misconstrued the term *neighbor*. To them, it meant only people of the same nationality and faith as they were. Although no verse in the Bible explicitly says we're to hate our neighbors, the Pharisees could and did reinterpret certain passages to justify doing just that (see Ps. 139:19-22; 140:9-11). In contrast, Jesus excluded hating anyone.

Jesus stated that the true intent of God's law was to challenge His people to love their enemies as well as their neighbors. This was difficult for those who, like the Pharisees, had a very narrow view of neighbor. Luke recorded one occasion when the Pharisees actually asked Jesus, "Who is my neighbor?" (Luke 10:29). Jesus responded with the parable of the good Samaritan. To the Pharisees, Jesus might as well have told them that their neighbors were people in leprosy camps. To the Jews, the Samaritans were the lowest of the low. Jesus gave this example to show that God's people are to love all people, not just their own. It was quite a radical idea in the culture of His day.

In Matthew 5:45 Jesus rebuffed the Jews who thought God was their Father alone. In explaining that their Father allows the sun to rise for all and the rain to fall on the righteous and the unrighteous, Jesus was saying that in one way or another, God the Father is caring and loving to all people, even those who rebel against Him. In the same way, we're to love all people.

If we don't love everyone, even enemies, Jesus said we're no different from people who don't know God (see vv. 46-48). This unconditional, holy love is characteristic of the kingdom of heaven.

How do you relate to a person who holds different political, philosophical, or religious views from yours? How do you maintain a warm relationship with a fellow believer with whom you differ?

› OBEY THE TEXT

God's Word governs the hearts of His people. As followers of Christ, we're called to live to a higher standard. Not only are we called to love other believers in Jesus; we're also called to love all, even our enemies.

What are some ways you're personally showing love to those whom others might not love? Think about your coworkers, classmates, and so on.

Because believers in Christ are called to a higher standard, list some ways your group can show love to your neighbors. Identify a group or individuals you'll commit to serve by loving them.

Discuss as a group how can you encourage one another to show others God's love. Put in place actions based on your discussion.

What are some ways you can challenge your Bible-study group to strive toward a higher standard of righteousness than that reflected by the world today? What agreements need to be made among group members to accomplish this? Discuss these agreements as a group and establish a group agreement.

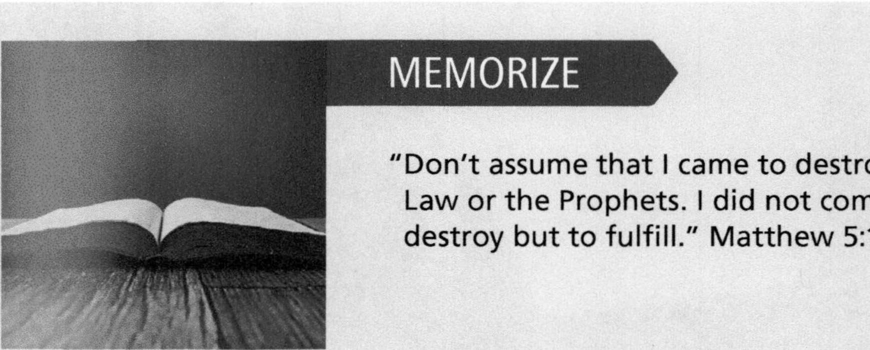

USE THE SPACE PROVIDED TO MAKE OBSERVATIONS AND RECORD PRAYER REQUESTS DURING THE GROUP EXPERIENCE FOR THIS SESSION.

MY THOUGHTS

Record insights and questions from the group experience.

MY RESPONSE

Note specific ways you'll put into practice the truth explored this week.

MY PRAYERS

List specific prayer needs and answers to remember this week.

SESSION 4

HOW TO GIVE, PRAY, & FAST

Spiritual disciplines seek a greater reward than this world can offer.

UNDERSTAND THE CONTEXT

USE THE FOLLOWING PAGES TO PREPARE FOR YOUR GROUP TIME.

Religion in Jesus' day was more a performance than a personal relationship with God. This was especially true in the practice of prayer. Jesus' disciples were accustomed to observing the Pharisees and scribes make a show of their faith through their public prayers. They weren't praying to communicate with and worship God but to be noticed by the common folk who saw and heard them praying in the marketplace.

In the first half of Matthew 6, Jesus focused on three areas of spiritual life: giving (see vv. 2-4), prayer (see vv. 5-15), and fasting (see vv. 16-18). When God's people engage in these activities, they should do so to glorify God. The motive behind any act of Christian service comes first and foremost under God's scrutiny. A good test to which believers should subject every outward expression of their faith is to ask, "If no one ever knew I did this, would I still do it?"

As Jesus delivered the Sermon on the Mount, He and His disciples were far from Jerusalem and the temple, but the disciples were familiar with His description of the prayer conduct of the religious leaders. No doubt they'd often watched that pretentious display of piety on the part of these men whom Jesus called hypocrites. They were making a mockery of one of the most sacred acts of worship toward God that a person could express. Throughout His earthly ministry, Jesus Himself often withdrew to a private place to pray. Spiritual strength and wisdom flowed into His being as a result of these regular encounters with His Father.

"IT IS NOT THE BODY'S POSTURE, BUT THE HEART'S ATTITUDE THAT COUNTS WHEN WE PRAY."

—Billy Graham

Think About It

Observe the various ways people approach God in prayer.

Identify the attitudes God desires behind our acts of devotion.

MATTHEW 6:1-18

1 Be careful not to practice your righteousness in front of people,
to be seen by them. Otherwise, you will have no reward from your
Father in heaven. **2** So whenever you give to the poor, don't sound
a trumpet before you, as the hypocrites do in the synagogues and
on the streets, to be applauded by people. I assure you: They've got
their reward! **3** But when you give to the poor, don't let your left
hand know what your right hand is doing, **4** so that your giving
may be in secret. And your Father who sees in secret will reward
you. **5** Whenever you pray, you must not be like the hypocrites,
because they love to pray standing in the synagogues and on the
street corners to be seen by people. I assure you: They've got their
reward! **6** But when you pray, go into your private room, shut your
door, and pray to your Father who is in secret. And your Father who
sees in secret will reward you. **7** When you pray, don't babble like
the idolaters, since they imagine they'll be heard for their many
words. **8** Don't be like them, because your Father knows the things
you need before you ask Him. **9** Therefore, you should pray like this:

> Our Father in heaven,
> Your name be honored as holy.
> **10** Your kingdom come.
> Your will be done
> on earth as it is in heaven.
> **11** Give us today our daily bread.
> **12** And forgive us our debts,
> as we also have forgiven our debtors.
> **13** And do not bring us into temptation,
> but deliver us from the evil one.
> [For Yours is the kingdom and the power
> and the glory forever. Amen.]

14 For if you forgive people their wrongdoing, your heavenly
Father will forgive you as well. **15** But if you don't forgive people,
your Father will not forgive your wrongdoing. **16** Whenever you
fast, don't be sad-faced like the hypocrites. For they make their
faces unattractive so their fasting is obvious to people. I assure
you: They've got their reward! **17** But when you fast, put oil on your
head, and wash your face, **18** so that you don't show your fasting
to people but to your Father who is in secret. And your Father who
sees in secret will reward you.

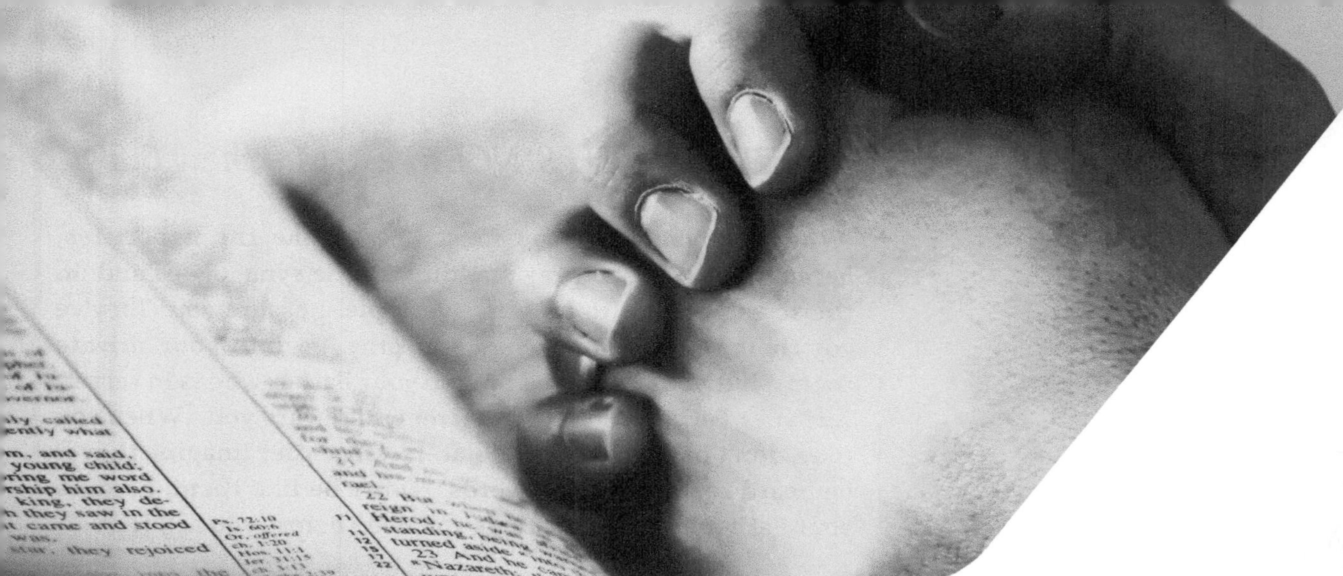

EXPLORE THE TEXT

GIVING FOR THE RIGHT REWARD (Matthew 6:1-4)

[1]Be careful not to practice your righteousness in front of people, to be seen by them. Otherwise, you will have no reward from your Father in heaven. [2]So whenever you give to the poor, don't sound a trumpet before you, as the hypocrites do in the synagogues and on the streets, to be applauded by people. I assure you: They've got their reward! [3]But when you give to the poor, don't let your left hand know what your right hand is doing, [4]so that your giving may be in secret. And your Father who sees in secret will reward you.

The first verse provides the key that unlocks the major theme of the following 17 verses. Jesus warned that righteous acts are to be done with the right motivation. Giving, praying, and fasting are all good deeds, but they can be done for the wrong reasons. It's interesting to note too that Jesus didn't instruct His disciples to do these things—it was understood that they'd do them. Rather, He instructed them on how to do them: whenever they give, pray, or fast.

Giving to God and caring for the poor have always been expected of God's people. These practices were characteristic of Israel (see Deut. 15:4-11; Mal. 3:7-12) and of the church (see Acts 4:32-35; 1 John 3:17-18). Jesus said giving to the poor—like any spiritual discipline—is a spiritual investment that has spiritual rewards. Giving financial resources can be a sacrifice, an act of obedience, worship, and love for God and for people made in His image. However, if the heart's desire is to earn human recognition, the action has an immediate return but no eternal value.

PRAYING WITH SINCERITY (Matthew 6:5-8)

[5]Whenever you pray, you must not be like the hypocrites, because they love to pray standing in the synagogues and on the street corners to be seen by people. I assure you: They've got their reward! [6]But when you pray, go into your private room, shut your door, and pray to your Father who is in secret. And your Father who sees in secret will reward you. [7]When you pray, don't babble like the idolaters, since they imagine they'll be heard for their many words. [8]Don't be like them, because your Father knows the things you need before you ask Him.

Prayer was an important part of Jewish religious life. Not only had the Jews been given God's written Word, but God had also communicated directly with Abraham and many of his descendants, and they'd felt free to speak to Him. But some in Jesus' day had allowed the privilege of prayer to be corrupted by rituals and human traditions.

Jesus condemned hypocritical prayer, not all public prayer. In this instance, however, Jesus was pointing out the importance of sincerity. In the secret place of prayer, the needs we share are for God's ears and not for others to hear. During those quiet times we're impressed with the certainty that God has heard us and will answer in accordance with His will. Some well-meaning Christians today may think repeating certain phrases over and over will move God to act on their behalf. Genuine prayer, however, doesn't seek to manipulate God. God responds to the righteous heart in sincere prayer, not to someone who utters empty words.

Jesus' statement that "your Father knows the things you need before you ask Him" (v. 8) poses something of a mystery concerning prayer. Why are we exhorted to pray if God already knows what we need and is able to meet those needs? Actually, when we pray, we're admitting to God our inability to meet our own needs. When we pray from the heart, we're exercising our faith and expressing our dependence on God. On the other hand, repeating those needs to Him again and again may reveal a lack of faith that God is listening to us and a belief that He must be cajoled or badgered into coming to our aid.

Do you find yourself using the same words or phrases often in your prayers? How could you freshen up your prayers by limiting the use of tired, worn-out phrases?

KEY DOCTRINE
God the Father

God as Father reigns with providential care over His universe, His creatures, and the flow of the stream of human history, according to the purposes of His grace.

A MODEL TO FOLLOW (Matthew 6:9-15)

9Therefore, you should pray like this:
Our Father in heaven,
Your name be honored as holy.
10Your kingdom come.
Your will be done
on earth as it is in heaven.

Prayer played a major role in Jesus' earthly life. He prayed with His disciples but also spent much time alone in prayer. The disciples were aware of Jesus' prayer habits, and one day one of them said to Him, "Lord, teach us to pray, just as John also taught his disciples" (Luke 11:1). He gave them a simple but comprehensive prayer outline as a model. He didn't specify a time; a place; or even a posture for prayer, whether standing, kneeling, looking up with outstretched hands, or bowing the head. Prayer is appropriate anytime, anyplace, and under any circumstance.

This model prayer has two parts. First, it addresses God's glory (see Matt. 6:9-10). Second, it considers people's need (see vv. 11-13a). Jesus combined praise for a majestic, awesome God (in heaven) with supplication from a loving, approachable God (our Father). His name is hallowed and to be honored above all other names. God's ultimate purpose is for His kingdom to be established on earth so that His will can be accomplished. This implies the total surrender of our will to the perfect will of God.

What commitments are evident in the way God is addressed in these verses? What commitments should we make when we approach God with our requests?

BIBLE SKILL
Use a Bible dictionary (either print or online) to research religious practices mentioned in Scripture.

The Jews of the first century placed a major emphasis on religious practices such as fasting and prayer. Read articles about fasting and prayer in a Bible dictionary. Give attention to the origins of those practices in Judaism and ways they changed over time.

11Give us today our daily bread.
12And forgive us our debts,
as we also have forgiven our debtors.

In these verses Jesus had our personal needs in mind. In the first century people were typically paid daily and immediately went to buy the family's food. The Greek word translated *daily* (see v. 11), which appears only here in the New Testament, is rich in meaning. It points to God's provision for each day, reminding us of the daily provision of manna for the Israelites in the wilderness (see Ex. 16:15-26). Our continual need for bread is comparable to our daily need for God.

The word translated *debts* in Matthew 6:12 is one of several New Testament words for *sin*. Jesus wasn't saying that God's forgiveness of our sin is dependent on our willingness to forgive others. Rather, those who understand the greatness of God's forgiveness they've received should gladly extend forgiveness to those who've wronged them. Jesus expanded on this truth in verses 14-15.

13And do not bring us into temptation,
but deliver us from the evil one.
[For Yours is the kingdom and the power
and the glory forever. Amen.]

14For if you forgive people their wrongdoing, your heavenly Father will forgive you as well. 15But if you don't forgive people, your Father will not forgive your wrongdoing.

God allows temptation, but He's never the author of temptation (see Jas. 1:13). The sense of Jesus' teaching in Matthew 6:13 may be "Don't let us surrender to temptation." God may allow us to be tested by temptation, but His testing is for a purpose (see 1 Cor. 10:13).

The closing doxology in Matthew 6:13 declares God's preeminence as reflected in His eternal kingdom, as well as His absolute power and glory, which are worthy of our praise.

How can a model prayer be helpful? What are the dangers? How would you describe Jesus' purpose in providing this model prayer?

FASTING WITH JOY *(Matthew 6:16-18)*

[16]Whenever you fast, don't be sad-faced like the hypocrites. For they make their faces unattractive so their fasting is obvious to people. I assure you: They've got their reward! [17]But when you fast, put oil on your head, and wash your face, [18]so that you don't show your fasting to people but to your Father who is in secret. And your Father who sees in secret will reward you.

The religious leaders had been hypocritical in their giving, in their praying, and in their fasting. Fasting is modeled in the New Testament. Jesus Himself fasted (see Matt. 4:2), Paul fasted (see Acts 9:9), and the early church fasted (Acts 13:2). Fasting is a valuable spiritual discipline when we focus our minds on God and seek a deeper prayer experience with Him. The Pharisees fasted twice a week (see Luke 18:12) but for all the wrong reasons. Instead of using these fasting days as times for genuine prayer and for searching their hearts, they saw them as opportunities to impress people with their piety and spirituality. Jesus clearly expected His disciples to fast, but He warned them against doing it to parade their holiness before others.

How can fasting be used and misused in a Christian's life? How can a person fast in practical ways without making it known? What are some life experiences that fasting could help?

› **OBEY** THE TEXT

Spiritual disciplines seek a greater reward than this world can offer. When we pray, we're to approach God with reverence and humility. We should view prayer as a conversation with the holy God for the purpose of understanding His heart and will. We must examine our motives for giving, praying, and fasting, remaining alert to prideful, self-righteous attitudes.

Identify the steps you take to prepare yourself to approach God in prayer. What changes do you need to make in light of this passage?

Evaluate your motives behind your prayer habits. How do your prayer requests reflect the model prayer presented by Jesus? What do you need to add to your prayer list to align your prayers with Jesus' example?

Discuss how group members can follow the principles revealed in this passage. List actions the group needs to take to maintain a meaningful prayer life.

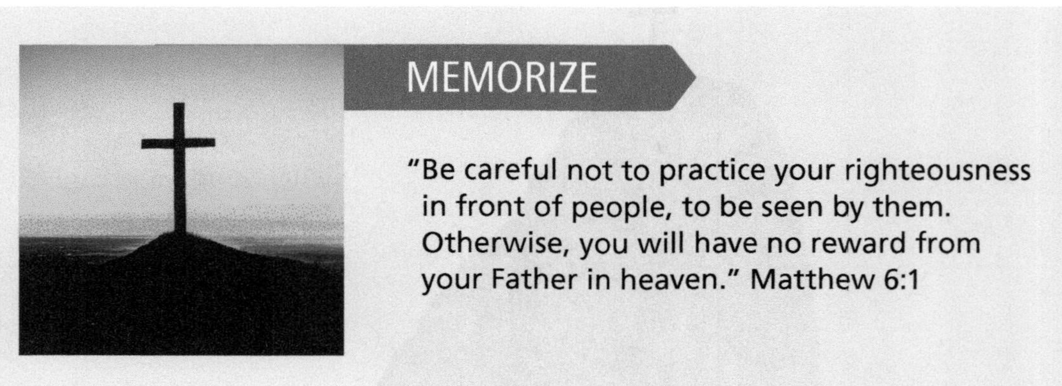

MEMORIZE

"Be careful not to practice your righteousness in front of people, to be seen by them. Otherwise, you will have no reward from your Father in heaven." Matthew 6:1

USE THE SPACE PROVIDED TO MAKE OBSERVATIONS AND RECORD PRAYER REQUESTS DURING THE GROUP EXPERIENCE FOR THIS SESSION.

MY THOUGHTS

Record insights and questions from the group experience.

MY RESPONSE

Note specific ways you'll put into practice the truth explored this week.

MY PRAYERS

List specific prayer needs and answers to remember this week.

Earthly & Eternal Concerns

Kingdom-minded people can live in freedom and peace.

UNDERSTAND THE CONTEXT

USE THE FOLLOWING PAGES TO PREPARE FOR YOUR GROUP TIME.

Never one to shy away from tough truths, during the Sermon on the Mount Jesus challenged the ethos of the culture of the time (arguably, the ethos of cultures throughout time): materialism. Regardless of our social strata or material wealth, people consistently seem concerned with gaining more possessions. Sin has taught us to focus on temporary, material things to the detriment of our concern for eternal, spiritual things.

Self-preservation is a human instinct that has long been used by the Enemy to twist people's hearts toward selfishness and materialism. If he can keep us worrying about ourselves, he can keep our minds off God's kingdom and the needs of others. Even the religious leaders of Jesus' time seemed to fall for this ruse and were "full of greed and self-indulgence," as He asserted in Matthew 23:25. During the Sermon on the Mount Jesus confronted this spirit of materialism head-on.

True to His fashion, the Lord introduced a radically countercultural principle. In a culture where people were fighting to survive and clawing to get ahead, Jesus stood before His audience and instructed them to stop chasing wealth and discontinue their worry over daily needs. Instead, He called the people to concern themselves with the things of God. He encouraged them to abandon their short view of life, which consisted of material concerns. Instead, He encouraged them to adopt the long view and live for God's kingdom, seeking His righteousness and storing up treasure in heaven.

Matthew 6:19-34 examines priorities in life. Jesus called for a right relationship between believers and material things. Material things threaten allegiance to God. Christians can't have two masters. A person can treasure either God or money but not both. Jesus then summarized by calling on His followers to "seek first the kingdom of God and His righteousness" (v. 33).

"WORRY DOES NOT EMPTY TOMORROW OF ITS SORROW, IT EMPTIES TODAY OF ITS STRENGTH."

—Corrie ten Boom

› MATTHEW 6:19-34

Think About It

Identify and answer the questions Jesus asked in this passage.

19 Don't collect for yourselves treasures on earth, where moth and rust destroy and where thieves break in and steal. **20** But collect for yourselves treasures in heaven, where neither moth nor rust destroys, and where thieves don't break in and steal. **21** For where your treasure is, there your heart will be also. **22** The eye is the lamp of the body. If your eye is good, your whole body will be full of light. **23** But if your eye is bad, your whole body will be full of darkness. So if the light within you is darkness—how deep is that darkness! **24** No one can be a slave of two masters, since either he will hate one and love the other, or be devoted to one and despise the other. You cannot be slaves of God and of money. **25** This is why I tell you: Don't worry about your life, what you will eat or what you will drink; or about your body, what you will wear. Isn't life more than food and the body more than clothing? **26** Look at the birds of the sky: They don't sow or reap or gather into barns, yet your heavenly Father feeds them. Aren't you worth more than they? **27** Can any of you add a single cubit to his height by worrying? **28** And why do you worry about clothes? Learn how the wildflowers of the field grow: they don't labor or spin thread. **29** Yet I tell you that not even Solomon in all his splendor was adorned like one of these! **30** If that's how God clothes the grass of the field, which is here today and thrown into the furnace tomorrow, won't He do much more for you—you of little faith? **31** So don't worry, saying, "What will we eat?" or "What will we drink?" or "What will we wear?" **32** For the idolaters eagerly seek all these things, and your heavenly Father knows that you need them. **33** But seek first the kingdom of God and His righteousness, and all these things will be provided for you. **34** Therefore don't worry about tomorrow, because tomorrow will worry about itself. Each day has enough trouble of its own.

EXPLORE THE TEXT

TREASURES ON EARTH AND IN HEAVEN (Matthew 6:19-21)

**19Don't collect for yourselves treasures on earth, where moth and rust destroy
and where thieves break in and steal. 20But collect for yourselves treasures
in heaven, where neither moth nor rust destroys, and where thieves don't
break in and steal. 21For where your treasure is, there your heart will be also.**

We have two options: collect treasures on earth or in heaven. And where these treasures are collected, whether in heaven or on earth, has everything to do with what kinds of treasures we're collecting. Material treasures remain here on earth where everything is at risk of theft and where everything will one day be destroyed. Treasures collected in heaven, on the other hand, are immaterial. Unlike physical possessions, the treasures of heaven consist of acts of righteousness and a life of holiness—essentially, anything that has Kingdom value in the eyes of the Father. Earthly treasures may offer pleasure in the moment, but they're of no value in eternity. In contrast, heavenly treasures are a pleasure both now and, to an incalculably greater extent, forevermore in eternity.

So the types of treasures you collect determines where those treasures are collected, and where your treasures are collected determines where your heart is. People who are consumed with collecting treasures on earth don't have their hearts set on heaven. History offers us examples of people who abandoned their treasures on earth to collect treasure in heaven. Professional athletes have abandoned million-dollar contracts in their prime, business people have given up high salaries at lucrative jobs, and the original disciples left their jobs and homes to follow Jesus. These are stellar examples of what it looks like to collect treasures in heaven.

If people looked at your life to identify where your treasures are collected, what would they say? Why?

THE GOOD EYE AND THE BAD EYE (Matthew 6:22-23)

22The eye is the lamp of the body. If your eye is good, your whole body will be full of light. 23But if your eye is bad, your whole body will be full of darkness. So if the light within you is darkness—how deep is that darkness!

Jesus compared the eye to a lamp. Just as a lamp fills a room with light, the eye fills the body with light. According to Jesus, your eye can be good—that is, clear—or it can be bad. If your eye is clear, you'll be filled with light. However, if your eye is bad, your whole body will be full of darkness. This image might seem confusing, but the fact that these two verses are couched between Jesus' teaching on treasure and wealth, respectively, might hint at what Jesus had in mind.

The eye isn't a source of light by itself. We see with our eyes, but we also see by the light that illuminates what's around us. Light is routinely associated with purity and holiness throughout Scripture. If our attention is fixed on pure and holy things, that light will fill our lives. Darkness, on the other hand, is consistently associated with sin and evil throughout Scripture. So if our eyes are fixed on selfish ambition, greed, and the treasures of this earth, our whole lives will be filled with that darkness. In essence, clear eyes look heavenward, but dark eyes are consumed with the material concerns of earth.

What are some of the things you concern yourself with on a daily basis?

How do these things fill your life with either light or darkness?

KEY DOCTRINE
The Kingdom

Christians ought to pray and to labor that the Kingdom may come and God's will be done on earth.

TWO MASTERS (Matthew 6:24-34)

[24]No one can be a slave of two masters, since either he will hate one and love the other, or be devoted to one and despise the other. You cannot be slaves of God and of money.

When it comes to serving multiple masters, one master will always stand above the rest. The meaning of the Greek word used here for *hate* is *to pursue with hatred,* whereas *love* means *to welcome and love dearly.* So Jesus wasn't describing a passive favoring of one master over the other. The reality is, when we attempt to serve two masters, we inevitably come to the point where we lovingly welcome one master deeper into our lives while chasing the other out of our lives.

To love God above all else doesn't mean we hate everything else. Rather, it means our love for God is so stratospherically above every other affection that it makes every other affection look closer to hatred in comparison. In verse 24 Jesus asserted that we can't serve God and money. We must serve God above everything else in our lives, including our wealth, and we must serve Him with everything we have, holding nothing back, including our wealth.

What are the masters in your life that compete with God for your devotion?

DON'T WORRY (Matthew 6:25-34)

[25]This is why I tell you: Don't worry about your life, what you will eat or what you will drink; or about your body, what you will wear. Isn't life more than food and the body more than clothing? [26]Look at the birds of the sky: They don't sow or reap or gather into barns, yet your heavenly Father feeds them. Aren't you worth more than they? [27]Can any of you add

BIBLE SKILL
Read, reflect on, and emotionally react to a Bible verse.

Read Matthew 6:33 aloud several times, emphasizing different words or phrases each time you read. For example, in one reading emphasize "Seek first." In the next reading emphasize what Jesus said to seek. In the next reading emphasize His promise to those who seek it. Finally, emphasize the name of and pronouns for God. Take notes on your thoughts.

How does the verse move you emotionally? What feelings were evoked by the different words and phrases as you emphasized them?

a single cubit to his height by worrying? 28And why do you
worry about clothes? Learn how the wildflowers of the field
grow: they don't labor or spin thread. 29Yet I tell you that
not even Solomon in all his splendor was adorned like one of
these! 30If that's how God clothes the grass of the field, which
is here today and thrown into the furnace tomorrow, won't He
do much more for you—you of little faith? 31So don't worry,
saying, "What will we eat?" or "What will we drink?" or "What
will we wear?" 32For the idolaters eagerly seek all these things,
and your heavenly Father knows that you need them. 33But
seek first the kingdom of God and His righteousness, and all
these things will be provided for you. 34Therefore don't worry
about tomorrow, because tomorrow will worry about itself.
Each day has enough trouble of its own.

In this passage Jesus traced worry back to the most basic human needs: food, drink, and clothing. Everyone on earth is concerned about these things, to some degree or another. The poor and rich alike concern themselves with food to fill their bellies, drink to slake their thirsts, and clothes to protect their bodies from the elements. There's no shame in having a pragmatic concern with the necessities of life, but when we worry, we reveal a shortage of faith.

Worry is born when we obsessively focus our attentions on something, forgetting that life is about more than the subject of our concerns. Here Jesus reminded us that life is more than food, drink, and clothes. Do we need these things to survive? Yes, but the more necessary something is to life, the more imperative it is that we entrust it to God.

At this point Jesus directed the crowd's attention to the birds flying overhead and the lilies at their feet. All creation depends on God for survival. If He ignored the needs of His creation, we'd have bald fields and empty skies, the lilies and birds having long died off. Let's look at God's flourishing creation and remember that there's no such thing as divine neglect. God would no more forget to provide for your basic needs than good parents would forget to feed their crying infant.

It was never Jesus' intention to come to earth and simply provide us with a list of things not to do. In these verses He isn't simply concerned with taking away our worry over the basic needs of the body. His intention is to replace worry with a higher concern for God's kingdom and righteousness.

What are some negative consequences of allowing worry to rule in our lives?

What might it look like to seek God's kingdom and righteousness in our daily lives?

› OBEY THE TEXT

Kingdom-minded people can live in freedom and peace. When our focus is on serving Christ in righteousness, then the things of this world have no power over us. We are satisfied perfectly in our relationship with our Heavenly Father who provides everything we need in His love for us.

What earthly treasures tempt you toward distraction from heavenly treasures?

Why is it important that we have no other master alongside God in our lives? What measures can you take to safeguard your faithfulness to God as your only Master?

How have you seen God's work in your life during moments of anxiety? In what ways can you intentionally try to worry less about the things of the world and instead seek God's kingdom and righteousness?

MEMORIZE

"Seek first the kingdom of God and His righteousness, and all these things will be provided for you." Matthew 6:33

USE THE SPACE PROVIDED TO MAKE OBSERVATIONS AND RECORD PRAYER REQUESTS DURING THE GROUP EXPERIENCE FOR THIS SESSION.

MY THOUGHTS

Record insights and questions from the group experience.

MY RESPONSE

Note specific ways you'll put into practice the truth explored this week.

MY PRAYERS

List specific prayer needs and answers to remember this week.

TWO GATES, ROADS, & FOUNDATIONS

Every person faces a choice about his or her life now and forever.

UNDERSTAND THE CONTEXT

USE THE FOLLOWING PAGES TO PREPARE FOR YOUR GROUP TIME.

In His conclusion to the Sermon on the Mount, Jesus issued a series of commands. In Matthew 7:1 He commanded, "Do not judge." In verse 6 He commanded His followers to be discerning about what's sacred and precious. He followed with a familiar command in verses 7-11 that we should be persistent in prayer. In verse 12 He gave the command to practice what we call the Golden Rule.

As is true of the sermon as a whole, the point in this passage isn't so much about how a person enters God's kingdom as it is about how those who've entered it should live as kingdom citizens. In the middle of this section, Jesus spoke about entering the kingdom in terms of its gate, its way, its population, and its destination. He highlighted these features by describing the alternative gate, way, population, and destination (see vv. 13-14).

In warning about false prophets (see vv. 15-23), Jesus pointed to the quality of a prophet's life as his credentials. Eloquence, persuasiveness, attractive personalities, popular followings, and powerful deeds aren't the best indicators of genuine spokespersons for God. In putting the focus on a prophet's manner of life, Jesus introduced another contrast studied previously, one between good fruit and bad fruit.

Jesus ended the sermon in verses 24-27 by contrasting people who merely hear His words with those who not only hear them but also put them into practice. A world of difference exists between hearing truth and practicing truth. The sermon's impact is recorded in verses 28-29. The crowds perceived that Jesus spoke with uncommon authority.

"TWO ROADS DIVERGED IN A WOOD, AND I— I TOOK THE ONE LESS TRAVELED BY, AND THAT HAS MADE ALL THE DIFFERENCE."

—Robert Frost

› MATTHEW 7:13-14,21-29

Think About It

Notice the common factors in the two houses.

How do the similarities magnify the differences?

13 "Enter through the narrow gate. For the gate is wide and the road is broad that leads to destruction, and there are many who go through it. **14** How narrow is the gate and difficult the road that leads to life, and few find it.

21 "Not everyone who says to Me, 'Lord, Lord!' will enter the kingdom of heaven, but only the one who does the will of My Father in heaven. **22** On that day many will say to Me, 'Lord, Lord, didn't we prophesy in Your name, drive out demons in Your name, and do many miracles in Your name?' **23** Then I will announce to them, 'I never knew you! Depart from Me, you lawbreakers!' **24** Therefore, everyone who hears these words of Mine and acts on them will be like a sensible man who built his house on the rock. **25** The rain fell, the rivers rose, and the winds blew and pounded that house. Yet it didn't collapse, because its foundation was on the rock. **26** But everyone who hears these words of Mine and doesn't act on them will be like a foolish man who built his house on the sand. **27** The rain fell, the rivers rose, the winds blew and pounded that house, and it collapsed. And its collapse was great!" **28** When Jesus had finished this sermon, the crowds were astonished at His teaching, **29** because He was teaching them like one who had authority, and not like their scribes.

EXPLORE THE TEXT

NARROW VERSUS WIDE (Matthew 7:13-14)

13Enter through the narrow gate. For the gate is wide and the road is broad that leads to destruction, and there are many who go through it. 14How narrow is the gate and difficult the road that leads to life, and few find it.

Jesus likened the choice facing His hearers to the choice between a narrow gate and a broad gate. Before describing the better way of the narrow gate, He wanted people to understand clearly where the alternative path leads. He described the destination lying at the end of the broad road as destruction. We aren't to think of destruction as annihilation or ceasing to exist. Rather, this word translates a term that has the basic meaning of suffering loss. The end of a life lived on the broad, popular road is the loss of all that's good and valuable—the loss of joy and fulfillment in eternity. In Matthew 16:26 Jesus pointed out the poor judgment of gaining the world but losing one's own life. The easy way is the most popular way. The way that seems right to the majority is in fact the way to death (see Prov. 14:12).

In Matthew 7:13 Jesus described the way beyond the wide gate as a broad road. In verse 14 He described the way beyond the narrow gate. The word *narrow* in this verse comes from a verb meaning *to experience trouble*. Jesus wants His followers to know that the way of a disciple is demanding, not easy. It requires discipline and dedication. Its difficult demands make it the choice of the few, not the many. However, the end of the difficult path makes it all worthwhile. It leads not to destruction or loss but to life.

This passage speaks to us about the initial decision to reject all other imagined ways to begin the Christian life in favor of faith in Christ alone. Furthermore, the passage also refers to the disciplined, demanding life that continues to make daily, self-denying choices in order to remain obedient to Jesus' commands.

How might Jesus' words influence the way we view our family members, friends, and coworkers?

Is there a qualitative difference between the way we live our lives and the way they live their lives?

KNOWN VERSUS UNKNOWN
(Matthew 7:21-23)

21Not everyone who says to Me, "Lord, Lord!" will enter the kingdom of heaven, but only the one who does the will of My Father in heaven. 22On that day many will say to Me, "Lord, Lord, didn't we prophesy in Your name, drive out demons in Your name, and do many miracles in Your name?" 23Then I will announce to them, "I never knew you! Depart from Me, you lawbreakers!"

Jesus declared that people whose claims to be Christians are nothing more than outward appearances and empty words will find themselves outsiders to the kingdom of heaven. Some may even say all the right words, like "Lord, Lord!" (vv. 21-22). However, Jesus declared that a genuine relationship with Him is determined by the manner of a person's life, not by his or her vocabulary. The crucial test for kingdom citizens is doing the Lord's will, not speaking His name.

These verses provide the key for understanding the images Jesus used in the preceding and following verses. Doing the will of God is the gate and the path that lead into the kingdom of heaven. Children of God obey their Heavenly Father. Righteous actions don't earn the way into heaven; rather they're good fruit revealing a person's true nature. They're good deeds shining a light before others so that they can see our Father in heaven (see Matt. 5:16). Righteousness is foundational to life in the kingdom of God.

KEY DOCTRINE
Judgment

According to His promise, Jesus Christ will return personally and visibly in glory to the earth. The dead will be raised, and Christ will judge all people in righteousness.

What are you doing to develop your personal relationship with Jesus? How are you spending time getting to know Him?

How can you check your motives to be sure your good deeds are done from your love for the Lord?

ROCK VERSUS SAND (*Matthew 7:24-29*)

24 Therefore, everyone who hears these words of Mine and acts on them will be like a sensible man who built his house on the rock. 25 The rain fell, the rivers rose, and the winds blew and pounded that house. Yet it didn't collapse, because its foundation was on the rock.

Jesus compared the choice facing His hearers with building a house on sand or on rock. The point of His warning is about building our lives on anything other than Him and His Word.

In describing the wise man, Jesus meant a person's spiritual condition, as opposed to the person's intellectual capacity. Ordinary wisdom dictates the need for a solid foundation for a house. Spiritual wisdom, on the other hand, dictates the need for building our lives on the solid rock of Christ. Jesus indicated that spiritual wisdom

BIBLE SKILL
Create a contrast chart to study a passage.

On one side of a vertical line, list all the words and phrases from Matthew 7:13-27 that are positive. On the other side of the line, list all the words or phrases that are negative. Use the chart to understand what the passage is saying about faithful obedience to Jesus.

has two dimensions: hearing His Word and acting on it. The absence of such wisdom results only in hearing His Word but stops short of acting on it.

Using the forces of nature to represent divine judgment, Jesus pointed out that falling rain, rising floods, and pounding winds can't destroy a house that rests on a solid foundation.

26 But everyone who hears these words of Mine and doesn't act on
them will be like a foolish man who built his house on the sand.
27 The rain fell, the rivers rose, the winds blew and pounded that
house, and it collapsed. And its collapse was great!

Jesus proceeded to give the alternative part of His analogy by referring to a house builder who chose sand for his foundation. He described such a builder as foolish, lacking spiritual discernment and therefore making unwise choices when presented with the truth about Jesus.

Using the identical description of nature's forces, Jesus described the collapse of the foolish builder's house when confronted with heavy rain, flooding rivers, and raging winds. He described the ruin not only as a collapse but also as a great collapse (see v. 27). Given the serious nature of the outcomes for a person's response to Christ and His Word, refusing to hear and act on revealed truth is nothing short of a great calamity.

How do the images that Jesus used help you grasp His message?

28 When Jesus had finished this sermon, the crowds were
astonished at His teaching, 29 because He was teaching them
like one who had authority, and not like their scribes.

The Sermon on the Mount concludes with this description of astonishment. The crowds that had gathered to hear Jesus realized that He was unlike any religious teacher they'd ever heard.

Although they didn't fully realize the divine nature of Jesus, people were beginning to see that He was no ordinary man. Jesus was more than a prophet or a rabbi. Just as God's people had recognized that the law given to Moses had divine authority, Jesus' audience recognized that His words had a unique authority. Jesus was greater than Moses or any other human used by God in history. He pointed to a greater salvation than the exodus and delivered a greater law than the commandments recorded on Mount Sinai. He described a greater kingdom than any earthly nation or power. Jesus was revealing the kingdom of heaven right before their eyes.

How has studying the Sermon on the Mount given you a new perspective on daily life as a citizen of the kingdom of God?

OBEY THE TEXT

Every person faces a choice about his or her life now and forever. Trusting in Jesus is the only way we can obtain real life. We'll be held accountable for the life we live and for the legacy we leave. Building our lives on anything other than Jesus leads to destruction—devastating, eternal consequences.

Do you know anyone who's wrestling with the crucial choice about his or her eternal destiny? If so, what actions could you take that would help them make the right choice?

Having entered the narrow gate into God's kingdom, what choices do you face in seeking to live a disciplined, committed life as you continue on the narrow road of godly devotion to Christ and His Word? List actions you'll take to stay on the right path.

Share ways your Bible-study group can minister in a positive, loving way to people who appear to be headed down the broad road toward destruction.

MEMORIZE

"Not everyone who says to Me, 'Lord, Lord!' will enter the kingdom of heaven, but only the one who does the will of My Father in heaven." Matthew 7:21

USE THE SPACE PROVIDED TO MAKE OBSERVATIONS AND RECORD PRAYER REQUESTS DURING THE GROUP EXPERIENCE FOR THIS SESSION.

MY THOUGHTS

Record insights and questions from the group experience.

MY RESPONSE

Note specific ways you'll put into practice the truth explored this week.

MY PRAYERS

List specific prayer needs and answers to remember this week.

GETTING STARTED

OPENING OPTIONS: Choose one of the following to open the group discussion.

WEEKLY QUOTATION DISCUSSION STARTER: "Happiness is not a goal; it is a by-product." —Eleanor Roosevelt

- What's your initial response to this week's quotation?
- What's your happiest memory?
- When have been disappointed to discover that something didn't make you as happy as you had expected?
- Today we'll see that Jesus spoke of happiness in a surprising way.

CREATIVE ACTIVITY: To prepare, identify your happiest memory. Secure a photo or another object that reminds you of that memory. When everyone has arrived, open your time together by briefly sharing your happiest memory, showing any object that may help tell your story. Then use the following to open your discussion.

- Everyone wants to be happy. What's your happiest memory?
- What currently makes you happy?
- What do you currently look forward to?
- Some people have a tendency to think happiness is nonspiritual or a less spiritual emotion. Jesus, however opened the Sermon on the Mount with an appeal to our natural desire for true happiness, both now and in the future.

UNDERSTAND THE CONTEXT

PROVIDE BACKGROUND: Briefly introduce members to Matthew 5–7 by pointing out the major themes and any information or ideas that will help them understand Matthew 5:1-12 (see pp. 7 and 9). Then, to help people personally connect today's context with the original context, use the following questions and statements.

- Why was it important for the original audience of Matthew's Gospel to see Jesus in light of the Old Testament? Why is it still important for readers today?
- As we begin our study of Jesus' famous Sermon on the Mount, pay attention to ways Jesus reshaped people's understanding of life in relationship with God.

EXPLORE THE TEXT

READ THE BIBLE: Ask a volunteer to read Matthew 5:1-12.

DISCUSS: Use the following questions to discuss group members' initial reactions to the text.

- In verse 1 why is it significant that the statement "He went up the mountain" had been used only in the Old Testament when God gave Moses the law for His people? In what ways was Jesus greater than Moses?
- In verses 3 and 10 the Beatitudes begin and end with "for the kingdom of heaven is theirs." What does this statement reveal about the kingdom?
- As you look at each Beatitude, identify ways Jesus' descriptions of kingdom people stand in stark contrast with earthly cultures. What description is most surprising?
- What key word appears in each characteristic of kingdom people? What does this repetition reveal about Jesus' main point?
- The word *blessed* can also be translated *happy*. In verses 4-9 why is it significant that Jesus described the reason for happiness as being rooted in the future? How does each future hope relate to present realities? In verse 12 how did Jesus point to the past for encouragement?
- What does this Scripture passage reveal about God's character? About natural human tendencies? About life in the kingdom?

NOTE: Provide ample time for group members to share responses and questions about the text. Don't feel pressured to prioritize the printed agenda over group members' personal experiences. If time allows, discuss responses to the questions in the personal reading.

OBEY THE TEXT

RESPOND: Foster an environment of openness and action. Help individuals apply biblical truth to specific areas of personal thought, attitude, and/or behavior.

- Notice the way Matthew 5 begins. How are you putting yourself in a teachable posture to listen to Jesus? Are you His disciple?
- Notice that the second half of each Beatitude begins with the word *for*. Which description is most encouraging to you personally? Why?
- Which of the Beatitudes is most convicting? How can you begin valuing what Jesus described in that particular Beatitude?

PRAY: Close by asking for humble, teachable hearts. Thank God for new life through faith in Jesus. Pray that each person will reflect the character of a citizen of the kingdom of heaven.

GETTING STARTED

OPENING OPTIONS: Choose one of the following to open the group discussion.

WEEKLY QUOTATION DISCUSSION STARTER: "Spiritually, many of us are not living completely in the light or in the dark. We've settled for a life at dusk."—Gregg Matte

- What's your initial response to this week's quotation?
- On a scale of 1 to 10, 1 being total darkness and 10 being glorious light, how would you describe your spiritual walk and why?
- Though we often settle for blurry lines, Jesus clearly distinguishes between what is and isn't a characteristic of His followers.

CREATIVE ACTIVITY: Prepare ahead of time by acquiring and examining some dollar bills of various denominations. Depending on the year and denomination, several identifying marks are easily recognized to distinguish legitimate and counterfeit money (see *www.wikihow.com/Detect-Counterfeit-US-Money*). Once the group arrives, begin by showing your bills and prompting group members to examine bills in their possession. Then use the following questions and statements to open the discussion.

- How can you distinguish between true and counterfeit bills?
- Today we'll see how we can distinguish between what's true and false in relation to the kingdom of heaven.

UNDERSTAND THE CONTEXT

PROVIDE BACKGROUND: Briefly introduce today's Scriptures by pointing out the major themes and any information or ideas that will help group members understand Matthew 5:13-16; 7:15-20 (see p. 17). Then, to help people personally connect today's context with the original context, use the following questions and statements.

- What's the purpose of metaphors in communication?
- In this text Jesus used obvious physical realities to communicate sobering spiritual realities.

EXPLORE THE TEXT

READ THE BIBLE: Ask two volunteers to read Matthew 5:13-16; 7:15-20.

DISCUSS: Use the following questions to discuss group members' initial reactions to the text.

- What was salt used for in ancient times? Based on those functions, what purpose do Jesus' disciples serve on earth?
- What purpose does light serve in 5:14-15? What does this reveal about the Christian life?
- What did Jesus say about good works in 5:16? In 7:15-20?
- What's the relationship between a wolf and a sheep? How does that picture in 7:15 illustrate a serious warning for true disciples?
- Based on what Jesus said about tasteless salt in 5:13, hidden light in 5:15, and bad fruit in 7:16-20, how would Jesus respond to someone who claims to be a Christian but doesn't live like one?
- What do these Scripture passages reveal about God's character? About natural human tendencies? About life in the kingdom?

NOTE: Provide ample time for group members to share responses and questions about the text. Don't feel pressured to prioritize the printed agenda over group members' personal experiences. If time allows, discuss responses to the questions in the personal reading.

OBEY THE TEXT

RESPOND: Foster an environment of openness and action. Help individuals apply biblical truth to specific areas of personal thought, attitude, and/or behavior.

- In what specific ways have you been encouraged to glorify God by someone's good example?
- When have you hidden your light? When are you most tempted to hide your light?
- Is your life bearing good or bad fruit? What bad fruit needs to be uprooted?
- Is there someone in your life consistently bearing bad fruit whom you need to relate to differently and/or pray for differently?
- How will you live to help others see God instead of drawing attention to yourself?

PRAY: Close by praying that you'll boldly shine the light of Jesus for everyone around you to see. Ask for conviction to overcome any tendency to hide truth that may save someone else. Praise God for His goodness in saving you and for welcoming you into His kingdom. Pray for discernment in making the most of your time on earth before spending eternity in heaven.

GETTING STARTED

OPENING OPTIONS: Choose one of the following to open the group discussion.

WEEKLY QUOTATION DISCUSSION STARTER: "That old law about 'an eye for an eye' leaves everybody blind. The time is always right to do the right thing."—Martin Luther King Jr.

- What's your initial response to this week's quotation?
- How can a desire for something good, like justice, unintentionally harden hearts?
- Even though "eye for eye" (see Ex. 21:24) was originally a law intended to limit retaliation, not to encourage it, Jesus revealed that an emphasis on obeying the law had become a strict form of legalism that missed the point.

CREATIVE ACTIVITY: When the group has gathered, begin by pointing out that everyone has benefited from transportation in their lives and probably today. Now, as if taking a driver's exam, ask everyone to help you brainstorm aloud as many traffic laws as your group can identify in the next couple of minutes. Then use the following to open the discussion.

- Why do traffic laws exist? What could happen if you intentionally broke these laws? What if you accidentally broke these laws?
- Knowing how serious the consequences can be—even a matter of life or death—will anyone choose to stop driving or using transportation in order to be safe? Why or why not?
- In Jesus' time religious leaders were so determined to keep the law that they had added extra laws so that nobody could even get close to breaking the God-given law. People were missing out on the joy, freedom, and benefit of a relationship with God in order to be sure they never broke any laws. But Jesus had something new to say to people.

UNDERSTAND THE CONTEXT

PROVIDE BACKGROUND: Briefly introduce today's Scriptures by pointing out the major themes and any information or ideas that will help group members understand Matthew 5:17-22,43-48 (see p. 27). Then, to help people personally connect today's context with the original context, use the following questions and statements.

- By the time of Jesus' earthly ministry, a relationship with God had essentially been reduced to observing a strict set of religious rules. How can a person faithfully observe religious activities but miss a relationship with God?
- What's another example of doing the right thing with the wrong intention or when your heart isn't in it?
- Today we'll see that Jesus doesn't simply want us to do the right things. He wants us to have the right heart.

EXPLORE THE TEXT

READ THE BIBLE: Ask two volunteers to read Matthew 5:17-22,43-48.

DISCUSS: Use the following questions to discuss group members' initial reactions to the text.

- How would you describe Jesus' view of Scripture, according to verses 17-19? How would you describe Scripture's relationship to Jesus?
- What did Jesus mean by His reference to destroying the Law or Prophets? By His reference to fulfilling them?
- How is true righteousness is more than just practicing and teaching commands (see v. 20)?
- In verses 21-22 what did Jesus teach about outward and inward expressions of sin? Why does God judge hidden attitudes of the heart as severely as sinful actions?
- According to verses 43-48, why must disciples of Jesus live differently from the world?
- How would a disciple benefit by following Jesus' commands in these difficult relationships? How would the enemy, neighbor, or brother benefit?
- What do these commands reveal about the value Jesus saw in individuals? In relationships?
- What do these Scripture passage reveal about God's character? About natural human tendencies? About life in the kingdom?

NOTE: Provide ample time for group members to share responses and questions about the text. Don't feel pressured to prioritize the printed agenda over group members' personal experiences. If time allows, discuss responses to the questions in the personal reading.

OBEY THE TEXT

RESPOND: Foster an environment of openness and action. Help individuals apply biblical truth to specific areas of personal thought, attitude, and/or behavior.

- Are you more prone to abuse grace—treating the law as if Jesus destroyed it—or to become legalistic—not seeing the law fulfilled in Jesus?
- How are you practicing and teaching the truths of Scripture?
- What can you do this week to love God and people instead of simply conforming to religious or moral expectations?

PRAY: Close by thanking God for revealing Himself through Scripture and ultimately through the gospel. Praise Him for His grace. Ask for passion to live righteously and wholeheartedly for Jesus.

GETTING STARTED

OPENING OPTIONS: Choose one of the following to open the group discussion.

WEEKLY QUOTATION DISCUSSION STARTER: "It is not the body's posture, but the heart's attitude that counts when we pray."—Billy Graham

- What's your initial response to this week's quotation?
- What are your earliest memories of prayer?
- Who taught you to pray, and what did they teach you?
- Today we'll look at what Jesus taught His disciples about prayer and other spiritual disciplines.

CREATIVE ACTIVITY: Prepare by securing an item or an image that represents your favorite hobby (for example, a golf club). When the group has gathered, begin by identifying your favorite hobby. Tell them that they too could enjoy your hobby if they remember two important things. Then provide one positive instruction and one negative action to avoid when practicing that hobby. Invite other members to share two instructions for their favorite activity. Then ask the group if it can guess what the hobby is. After a few people have shared, use the following to open the discussion.

- What did you learn about group members' interests?
- How did you decide what was most important to do and not to do when participating in the activity you shared?
- Today we'll see what Jesus taught His disciples to do and not to do in practicing several essential spiritual activities.

UNDERSTAND THE CONTEXT

PROVIDE BACKGROUND: Briefly introduce today's Scripture by pointing out the major themes and any information or ideas that will help group members understand Matthew 6:1-18 (see p. 37). Then, to help people personally connect today's context with the original context, use the following questions and statements.

- Jesus confronted religious activity that was performed solely for show. How can religion—even going to church or being a part of a small group—become a religious performance?
- When has your spiritual life become empty routine or merely an expression of a proud desire to be seen by others as religious and spiritual?
- A good test to which believers should subject every outward expression of their faith is to ask, "If no one ever knew I did this, would I still do it?"

EXPLORE THE TEXT

READ THE BIBLE: Ask a volunteer to read Matthew 6:1-18.

DISCUSS: Use the following questions to discuss group members' initial reactions to the text.

- How does verse 1 provide the key to unlocking Jesus' main point about the following spiritual disciplines?
- How would you summarize Jesus' teaching on giving in verses 2-4? What did He discourage? What did He encourage? Why are these teachings important?
- How would you summarize Jesus' teaching on prayer in verses 5-8? What did He discourage? What did He encourage? Why are these teachings important?
- Instead of expecting us to recite our prayers word for word, what categories for prayer did Jesus identify in verses 9-13?
- How would you summarize Jesus' teaching on fasting in verses 16-18? What did He discourage? What did He encourage? Why are these teachings important?
- Is the repeated promise of a reward surprising in this passage? In the context of what's been studied so far in the Sermon on the Mount, what did Jesus mean by reward?
- What does this Scripture passage reveal about God's character? About natural human tendencies? About life in the kingdom?

NOTE: Provide ample time for group members to share responses and questions about the text. Don't feel pressured to prioritize the printed agenda over group members' personal experiences. If time allows, discuss responses to the questions in the personal reading.

OBEY THE TEXT

RESPOND: Foster an environment of openness and action. Help individuals apply biblical truth to specific areas of personal thought, attitude, and/or behavior.

- What habits, routines, or practices help you maintain a healthy spiritual life, specifically in your giving, praying, and fasting?
- When have you been tempted "to practice your righteousness in front of people, to be seen by them" (6:1)? How does social media affect your desire to be noticed?
- What will you do to ensure healthy motivation in your personal acts of righteousness?

PRAY: Close by having the group pray aloud together the model prayer in Matthew 6:9-13.

GETTING STARTED

OPENING OPTIONS: Choose one of the following to open the group discussion.

WEEKLY QUOTATION DISCUSSION STARTER: "Worry does not empty tomorrow of its sorrow. It empties today of its strength."—Corrie ten Boom

- What's your initial response to this week's quotation?
- What was the cause of your most recent worry?
- Though some of us more than others, we all worry. Jesus spoke directly to the heart of our tendency to worry.

CREATIVE ACTIVITY: Prepare by identifying a treasured personal item or collection. When the group has arrived, share the reason the item has special value to you or why you're interested in collecting certain items. Then ask whether anyone else has a prized possession or an interesting collection. After allowing a few people to share, use the following to open the discussion.

- Where's the line between enjoying something in a healthy way and obsessing over it?
- When has an obsession caused anxiety or other unhealthy attitudes and behaviors?
- People naturally tend to obsess over, idolize, and worry about things we want. Jesus didn't condemn our tendency to value things or pursue things, but He did have clear words about checking our priorities so that we treasure and seek things that are of true, infinite value. He invites His disciples to experience real peace and freedom.

UNDERSTAND THE CONTEXT

PROVIDE BACKGROUND: Briefly introduce today's Scripture by pointing out the major themes and any information or ideas that will help group members understand Matthew 6:19-34 (see p. 47). Then, to help people personally connect today's context with the original context, use the following questions and statements.

- Why would Jesus take time to address money and mundane practical matters instead of sticking to matters that were obviously religious?
- Dividing life into spiritual and nonspiritual matters is a false dichotomy. Once again, Jesus revealed that our attitudes and behaviors, even toward so-called practical matters, are issues of the heart.

EXPLORE THE TEXT

READ THE BIBLE: Ask a volunteer to read Matthew 6:19-34.

DISCUSS: Use the following questions to discuss group members' initial reactions to the text.

- How did Jesus contrast earthly and eternal treasures in verses 19-20?
- What's the relationship between the human heart and treasure (see v. 21)? How can this be negative? Positive?
- How can anyone, no matter how rich or poor, be obsessed with and a slave of money?
- What did Jesus mean in verse 24 by saying that people can't serve God and money?
- What did Jesus say in verses 22-23 about the importance of our focus? In verses 25-34?
- What evidence did Jesus provide to support His command not to worry (see vv. 25-32)?
- What promise did Jesus make in verse 33 about the kingdom of heaven and our needs on earth?
- What does this Scripture passage reveal about God's character? About natural human tendencies? About life in the kingdom?

NOTE: Provide ample time for group members to share responses and questions about the text. Don't feel pressured to prioritize the printed agenda over group members' personal experiences. If time allows, discuss responses to the questions in the personal reading.

OBEY THE TEXT

RESPOND: Foster an environment of openness and action. Help individuals apply biblical truth to specific areas of personal thought, attitude, and/or behavior.

- What good treasures most often become idols, distracting your attention and affection from eternal things? How can you enjoy those things without their becoming idolatrous treasures?
- Which of the things Jesus mentioned are you most prone to worry about: money (possessions), food (health), or clothing (appearance)?
- What helps you keep your focus on God's goodness and trust His provision instead of worrying like someone who doesn't know God?
- How can you focus on seeking God's kingdom and His righteousness each day instead of worrying about the future?

PRAY: Close by thanking God for His loving, lavish, and gracious provision for you as His child. Ask your Heavenly Father to help you trust Him in all things and to value Him above all things.

GETTING STARTED

OPENING OPTIONS: Choose one of the following to open the group discussion.

WEEKLY QUOTATION DISCUSSION STARTER:

> Two roads diverged in a wood, and I—
> I took the one less traveled by,
> And that has made all the difference.
> —Robert Frost

- What's your initial response to this week's quotation?
- When has an unpopular choice worked out well for you? When has going along with the crowd proved to be a bad decision?
- Long before this poet, Jesus contrasted two roads, the less traveled making an eternal difference.

CREATIVE ACTIVITY: Before the group arrives, get a coin. Begin your time together by explaining that you'll flip the coin once for each person in the room, allowing him or her to call heads or tails while it's in the air. After everyone has had a turn, use the following to open discussion.

- How many answered correctly? How many were wrong? Is it possible to get it somewhat right?
- How many times did the coin land on heads? On tails? Did the coin ever land on its side?
- No matter how many times you flip a coin, it will never land on its side. Similarly, Jesus concluded the Sermon on the Mount in no uncertain terms: we're either part of the kingdom of heaven, or we aren't. There's no in-between. We either respond affirmatively to Him, or we don't. Fortunately, there's no guesswork involved.

UNDERSTAND THE CONTEXT

PROVIDE BACKGROUND: Briefly introduce today's Scripture by pointing out the major themes and any information or ideas that will help group members understand Matthew 7:13-14,21-29 (see p. 57). Then, to help people personally connect today's context with the original context, use the following questions and statements.

- As we get ready to conclude the Sermon on the Mount, how would you describe Jesus' primary message so far about life in the kingdom of heaven?
- How have Jesus' words challenged your ideas, attitudes, and behaviors these past several weeks?

EXPLORE THE TEXT

READ THE BIBLE: Ask two volunteers to read Matthew 7:13-14,21-29.

DISCUSS: Use the following questions to discuss group members' initial reactions to the text.

- What do the narrow gate and the difficult road represent in verses 13-14? The wide gate and the broad road?
- What did Jesus mean when He said many find destruction and few find life?
- According to verses 21-23, what won't gain a person entry to the kingdom of heaven? What's required to enter the kingdom?
- According to verses 24-27, two men faced storms but had different outcomes. Why?
- What's the distinction between a sensible and a foolish man in relation to Jesus' words? How does this teaching echo Jesus' point about the gates, roads, and entrance into the kingdom?
- What does these Scripture passages reveal about God's character? About natural human tendencies? About life in the kingdom?

NOTE: Provide ample time for group members to share responses and questions about the text. Don't feel pressured to prioritize the printed agenda over group members' personal experiences. If time allows, discuss responses to the questions in the personal reading.

OBEY THE TEXT

RESPOND: Foster an environment of openness and action. Help individuals apply biblical truth to specific areas of personal thought, attitude, and/or behavior.

- Have you built your life firmly on the Word of God? What are you doing to actively hear and obey Jesus?
- When has trusting God brought you through a difficult storm?
- When are you tempted to follow the crowd instead of doing what you know is right? How will you resolve to follow Jesus, even when the road is difficult and when few seem to go with you?
- Whom do you know on the broad road headed for destruction can you lead to life by inviting them to follow Jesus with you?
- How can this group help you along the difficult path of life in the kingdom of heaven?

PRAY: Close by asking God to help your hear and obey His words. Thank Him for the incomparable joy of a saving relationship with Christ through faith. Pray for endurance through storms and difficult seasons as you follow Him each day.

TIPS FOR LEADING A GROUP

PRAYERFULLY PREPARE

Prepare for each session by—

- **reviewing the weekly material and group questions ahead of time;**
- **praying for each person in the group.**

Ask the Holy Spirit to work through you and the group discussion to help people take steps toward Jesus each week as directed by God's Word.

MINIMIZE DISTRACTIONS

Create a comfortable environment. If group members are uncomfortable, they'll be distracted and therefore not engaged in the group experience. Plan ahead by taking into consideration—

- **seating;**
- **temperature;**
- **lighting;**
- **food or drink;**
- **surrounding noise;**
- **general cleanliness (put pets away if meeting in a home).**

At best, thoughtfulness and hospitality show guests and group members they're welcome and valued in whatever environment you choose to gather. At worst, people may never notice your effort, but they're also not distracted. Do everything in your ability to help people focus on what's most important: connecting with God, with the Bible, and with others.

INCLUDE OTHERS

Your goal is to foster a community in which people are welcome just as they are but encouraged to grow spiritually. Always be aware of opportunities to—

- **invite** new people to join your group;
- **include** any people who visit the group.

An inexpensive way to make first-time guests feel welcome or to invite people to get involved is to give them their own copies of this Bible-study book.

ENCOURAGE DISCUSSION

A good small group has the following characteristics.

- **Everyone participates.** Encourage everyone to ask questions, share responses, or read aloud.
- **No one dominates—not even the leader.** Be sure what you say takes up less than half of your time together as a group. Politely redirect discussion if anyone dominates.
- **Nobody is rushed through questions.** Don't feel that a moment of silence is a bad thing. People often need time to think about their responses to questions they've just heard or to gain courage to share what God is stirring in their hearts.
- **Input is affirmed and followed up.** Make sure you point out something true or helpful in a response. Don't just move on. Build personal connections with follow-up questions, asking how other people have experienced similar things or how a truth has shaped their understanding of God and the Scripture you're studying. People are less likely to speak up if they fear that you don't actually want to hear their answers or that you're looking for only a certain answer.
- **God and His Word are central.** Opinions and experiences can be helpful, but God has given us the truth. Trust Scripture to be the authority and God's Spirit to work in people's lives. You can't change anyone, but God can. Continually point people to the Word and to active steps of faith.

KEEP CONNECTING

Think of ways to connect with members during the week. Participation during the session is always improved when members spend time connecting with one another away from the session. The more people are comfortable with and involved in one another's lives, the more they'll look forward to being together. When people move beyond being friendly and in the same group to truly being friends who form a community, they come to each session eager to engage instead of merely attending.

Encourage group members with thoughts, commitments, or questions from the session by connecting through—

- **emails;**
- **texts;**
- **social media.**

When possible, build deeper friendships by planning or spontaneously inviting group members to join you outside your regularly scheduled group time for—

- **meals;**
- **fun activities;**
- **projects around your home, church, or community.**

› GROUP CONTACT INFORMATION

Name ______________________ Number ______________________

Email/social media ______________________

Name ______________________ Number ______________________

Email/social media ______________________

Name ______________________ Number ______________________

Email/social media ______________________

Name ______________________ Number ______________________

Email/social media ______________________

Name ______________________ Number ______________________

Email/social media ______________________

Name ______________________ Number ______________________

Email/social media ______________________

Name ______________________ Number ______________________

Email/social media ______________________

Name ______________________ Number ______________________

Email/social media ______________________

Name ______________________ Number ______________________

Email/social media ______________________

Name ______________________ Number ______________________

Email/social media ______________________

Name ______________________ Number ______________________

Email/social media ______________________